Honoring the Gift:
The American Association of Tissue Banks at 40

American Association of Tissue Banks®

Troupe Noonan

Copyright © 2016

American Association of Tissue Banks
All rights reserved. No part of the content of this book
may be reproduced without the written permission of

The American Association of Tissue Banks
8200 Greensboro Drive, Suite 320
McLean, Virginia 22102

ISBN: 978-0-9851585-8-3

LOC#: 2016911857

First Edition

Printed and Bound in the United States of America

10 9 8 7 6 5 4 3 2 1

Photo Credits: All photographs, unless otherwise noted, are courtesy
the American Association of Tissue Banks

Heritage Histories develops and publishes custom
histories for corporations, schools, clubs, institutions,
and families. For further information, contact:

HERITAGE HISTORIES

1289 Fordham Boulevard, Suite 271
Chapel Hill, North Carolina 27514
www.heritagehistories.com
tnoonan@heritagehistories.com; 919 616-5397

Noonan, Troupe

Dedication

Honoring the Gift: The American Association of Tissue Banks at 40 is dedicated to the hundreds of thousands of donors, family members, and loved ones who made the courageous decision to become donors or authorize donation. These selfless acts—many of them truly life-saving—have led to better health, improved mobility, and increased longevity for millions of patients.

The AATB Board Governors, on behalf of the AATB membership, the staff and the institutions accredited by AATB, wishes to extend its humble gratitude and sincere appreciation for your generosity and compassion.

We also wish to acknowledge the thousands of AATB volunteers who have made the organization what it is today. There is an old proverb that says, "We drink from wells that we did not dig, and we are warmed by fires that we did not build." This is truly the case in the tissue banking profession; the successes of today and the patients' lives that have been saved and enhanced are due in large part to the pioneers who created, nurtured, and enhanced AATB's growth.

To all those early leaders, we simply say, "Thank you."

Acknowledgments

An institutional history is always a group effort, and *Honoring the Gift: The American Association of Tissue Banks at 40* has been no different. At the AATB, Director of Communications Sarah Gray, with whom I first spoke about the project, was always clear and thoughtful in her directives. Administrative and Communications Coordinator Veronica Escalona has been tireless in providing me information and running down every question and request.

Senior Vice President of Policy Scott Brubaker—who is regarded worldwide as the oracle where tissue banking is concerned—lived up to his reputation by providing background, context, depth, and corrections on many fronts. And President and CEO Frank Wilton made many crisp definitive decisions that allowed the book to proceed. These four individuals, along with Certification Manager Sandie Henderson-Boncore and Director of Finance and Administration Kathy Crandall, read the narrative numerous times, sometimes late at night or on weekends or on vacation. Without their thoughtful feedback, this history would not have been possible.

Outside the AATB, many, many people not only granted me interviews, but remained available for additional questions, and reviewed their quotes and information in order to ensure accuracy. Collectively, these many individuals represent a comprehensive archive for the history of the AATB, and they were all most generous with their time.

There are always numerous people involved in the production process, but I need to mention two in particular. Working with me were editor Katie Fisher, without whose eagle eye I simply do not like to write, and designer

Acknowledgments

Sheri Heckel, who always not only goes above and beyond in terms of delivering on time, but also produces stunning quality at every stage. There is nothing like being able to count on people 100%.

The entire field of tissue banking is characterized by generosity and selflessness, and that is reflected in the people with whom I was privileged to work on this book. It has been an honor. I hope you enjoy it.

–Troupe Noonan

Acknowledgments

AATB gratefully acknowledges the support of the following organizations, without which Honoring the Gift would have been impossible to produce.

AlloSource
CryoLife
Medline Industries
UMTB- a Vivex Company

Exsurco Medical
Musculoskeletal Transplant Foundation (MTF)
RTI Surgical/RTI Donor Services

Acelity
Community Tissue Services (CTS)
Donor Alliance
LifeLink
LifeNet Health
Medtronic
MiMedx
VRL Laboratories

Axogen
Bone Bank Allografts (BBA)
CORE
Davis Wright Tremaine
Donor Network West
One Legacy

Table of Contents

Preface: Honoring the Gift I

Foreword: A Brief History III

Chapter One:
A Growing Need: Tissue Banking,
1949–1976 1

Chapter Two:
Setting the Standards: The Early Years of the AATB,
1976–1987 15

Chapter Three:
Challenges, Collaboration, and Contractors: Taking the Next Step,
1987–2000 31

Chapter Four:
Technology, Growth, Consolidation, and Globalization,
2000–Present 63

Epilogue: Looking Ahead 85

Appendix 91

Endnotes 92

Permissions 94

Index 95

Preface: Honoring the Gift

The earliest reference to tissue transplantation occurred almost 900 years ago, but wide practice only commenced in the middle of the 20th century. Indeed, as late as 1994, only 6,000 Americans were tissue donors at their deaths.[1]

As of 2007, more than 30,000 of the millions of people who die in the United States and Canada each year become tissue donors. In other words, the number of deceased donors has quintupled in the last quarter century. An AATB survey in 2013 revealed that donations led to more than 2.5 million allografts distributed by AATB-accredited tissue banks, including over 200,000 skin/dermis allografts, 1.7 million musculoskeletal (bone, cartilage, joint—both conventional and those utilizing medical devices) allografts, more than 200,000 soft tissue (ligament, tendon, fascia, pericardium, nerve, dura, cardiac tissue [heart valve, cardiac conduit]) allografts, and 3,592 vascular (vein, artery) allografts.[2]

There are also thousands of donations from living donors annually, including autologous tissue, reproductive tissue, surgical bone tissue, and birth tissues such as such as amnion, amniotic membrane, chorionic membrane, cord tissue, and amniotic fluid.

The story of tissue banking and the AATB is undoubtedly one of medical innovation, but more than that, it is a human story that begins with individual donors making a gift.

A Verger's Dream: Saints Cosmas and Damian Performing a Miraculous Cure by Transplantation of a Leg. Oil painting attributed to the Master of Los Balbases, ca. 1495.

Foreword: A Brief History

The Early History of Transplantation

The earliest mention of any form of tissue transplantation occurred in the 12th century in Aegea, in the Roman province of Syria, when twin brothers and physicians Cosmas and Damien (who were later canonized as saints) allegedly amputated a patient's leg and transplanted the leg of a recently deceased Ethiopian slave.[3] This legend was the subject of many medieval reports and paintings.

A half-millennium later, in 1668, Job van Meekeren, a Dutch surgeon who specialized in hand surgery, was credited with the first successful bone transplant, having repaired a soldier's severe cranial fracture by filling a hole in his skull with a piece of skull from a dog. When the church threatened excommunication for such witchcraft, Van Meekeren attempted to remove the graft, but it had successfully integrated with the soldier's tissue.

More than 200 years later, in 1878, the first human-to-human bone transplantation in aseptic conditions was performed by Dr. (later Sir) William MacEwen, an orthopedic surgeon at the Glasgow Royal Infirmary in Scotland. During his career, MacEwen undertook important research in bone growth, and used bone grafts successfully in the treatment of rickets and knee injuries.

Further advancements in the field of bone allografts continued throughout the early 20th century. In 1908, large bone allografts were acquired from amputated limbs and subsequently used to fill, for example, a bone gap resulting from osteomyelitis or tumor surgery; in 1910, refrigerated allograft bone was successfully transplanted after three weeks of storage; in 1911, thin slices of bone for transplantation were successfully refrigerated for later use; and in 1915 a bone graft from a father was used to fill the defect of spina bifida of his son.[4]

Skin grafting started its advance shortly after bone allografting. The first completely documented human tissue grafting was performed in 1870 by Swiss surgeon Dr. Jacques Reverdin.[5] In 1871, George Pollock used his own skin along with that of his patient for coverage of a burn wound. In 1881, skin from a cadaver was successfully used for the first time to treat a burn wound, and in 1903 a skin graft was refrigerated and shown to successfully retain cell viability for 3 to 14 days.[6]

The first widespread use of skin grafting occurred about 15 years later when Dr. Harold Gillies, a surgeon at Royal Army Medical Corps and, later, Queen's Hospital in London, dressed the burns of an English factory worker who had fallen into a vat of boiling water with skin offered by colleagues. Gillies subsequently pioneered plastic reconstruction of soldiers burned during World War I, and it became a somewhat common practice for people to offer their skin for friends who had been burned in some way. The first cryopreserved skin graft occurred in 1971.

Vascular transplants began in 1911 with Dr. Alexis Carrel, a French surgeon who joined blood vessels utilizing vessels from a deceased donor. The first frozen venous allograft occurred 41 years later, in 1955, in a femoral artery bypass. The first cryopreserved venous allograft was used in 1974.

In 1956, the first fresh heart valve allograft was placed into the descending aorta and then, seven years later, it was implanted into the cardiac position. In 1971, the first frozen heart valve was used as an allograft.

Reproductive transplantation began in 1895, when Robert Morris performed the first human ovarian graft.[7]

Development of Medical Instruments and New Techniques

Medical instruments for these practices were often developed by the physicians who used them. MacEwen, for instance, developed an early osteotome, a double-beveled chisel-like instrument for cutting bone. Until the early 1930s, skin grafts had customarily been cut by hand, a practice that required considerable skill. These grafts were also generally small and very thin, making them difficult to handle, especially when coverage of large areas was necessary. In the early 1930s, however, Dr. James Barrett Brown, chief of plastic surgery at St. Louis Children's Hospital in Missouri, successfully grafted skin from a woman onto her son, who had suffered a deep and likely terminal burn. By the end of the third week, the grafts had been completely absorbed, and the wound was much improved. Both patients survived.[8]

Dr. Brown's research showed that, when cut thicker and larger, recovery of allograft skin could result in good healing at the donor site. He used the term "split-thickness skin graft." Brown thus revolutionized concepts of skin grafting that remain in use today, a development whose ramifications touched the entire field of burn treatment, especially the care of thermal burn injuries. The first dermatome, a calibrated device for removing skin in a uniform, predetermined thickness, was designed in 1937 by Earl C. Padgett, Sr. The Reese dermatome, an improvement upon the original, was developed during World War II.

It was not until 1960 that Peter Medawar won a Nobel Prize for determining that rejection of foreign grafting material is an immunological response

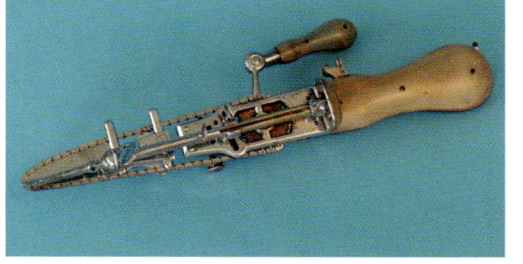
Osteotome

acquired before birth; surgeons had known for decades that skin taken from family members was better tolerated by the recipient than skin taken from strangers. Doctors were simply unable to predict if an unknown donor would belong to the same blood group as their patient. Familial skin was also the first choice in allografting because the considerable physical demands on the living donor rendered loving relatives far more likely than mere friends or strangers to agree to undergo the painful procedure.

Early Banking

Banking of human tissue likely began with the establishment of breast milk banking, which "grew in the early 1900's when wet nursing became less practical and the development of refrigeration and a greater knowledge of safe food processing allowed for pasteurization. The first milk bank in the United States was established in 1910 in Boston, MA."[9] Also in the early 1900s, various physicians froze and stored skin and bone grafts.[10]

Blood banking came next. In the late 1930s, Dr. Bernard Fantus of Chicago was the first person to seal and store blood in a refrigerator and successfully introduce it into a recipient. Fantus called his facility at Cook County Hospital a blood bank, a nickname that immediately became part of the popular vocabulary.

About the same time, during the Spanish Civil War (1936–39), doctors on both sides of the conflict were confronted by casualties on a mass scale. Consequently, the new technology of banked blood with extended shelf life was exploited to make blood available for the first time to large numbers of anticipated recipients, even those in an entirely different locale. This was called the "indirect" approach, as distinguished from the previously used "direct" approach, in which transfusions would be made be made one-on-one via the donor placing his or her arm directly against that of the recipient in order to avoid clotting caused by exposing the blood to air. Clearly, in the face of multiple casualties, the direct method was no longer practical.

Banks Proliferate, Pioneer Consent

World War II created a much wider need for donors than had the Spanish Civil War, and that need–combined with new technologies and practices–led to a new system of anonymous donation.

Though the early 20th century, European tissue banks likely utilized consent forms. In Europe, one of the earliest documented institutionalizations of consent for anonymous blood and tissue donation occurred at the Queen Victoria Hospital, a small cottage hospital in East Grinstead in the southeast corner of England, which began the practice of issuing pledge cards to people in the community who wished to be anonymous cornea and tissue donors. These cards were to be held separately from a last will and testament and read immediately after death, because the will was usually only read after burial or cremation—too late for recovering any form of tissue.

These pledge cards transferred responsibility by allowing people to authorize donation of their own transplantable tissues after their death, much as their wills gave instructions for the redistribution of personal effects like money, paintings, and jewelry. This circumvented the problem of family members refusing permission to recover the tissue, and led to the proliferation in the 1940s and 50s of hospital-based bone banks modeled on the blood bank system, where such donated tissue could be stored.

Like many medical advancements, early tissue banking was not without its critics, who argued that the practice reduced human bodies to impersonal resources for exchangeable and transplantable parts. The dissenters, however, could not outweigh the need, and after World War II, more and more small tissue banks began to appear at local hospitals around the country.[11]

Dr. George W. Hyatt

Chapter One:
A Growing Need: Tissue Banking, 1949–1976

A major shift from smaller, local tissue banks to larger regional ones was initiated in 1949 when Dr. George W. Hyatt, a Navy surgeon, was assigned, at his own request, to the orthopedic service at the U.S. Naval Hospital in Bethesda, Maryland. A graduate of Creighton University and its medical school, Dr. Hyatt had served in the Pacific during World War II. During a year's fellowship at the Navy's Lahey Clinic at Tufts, he had become interested in transplantation and conceived the idea of a Navy Tissue Bank, which he took to Congress.

According to Dr. William Tomford (AATB president, 1987–89), an orthopedic surgeon who served as director of the Navy Tissue Bank in the 1970s, Dr. Hyatt saw allograft tissue transplantation as a means for reconstruction of traumatic wartime injuries, and told Congress of his dream to be able to transplant a limb. A tissue bank, he told Congress, would be the first step.

"Of course replacing a limb was not realistic at that time," said Dr. Tomford; nonetheless, Congress felt that Dr. Hyatt's idea should be funded, so for many years the Department of Defense funded the Navy Tissue Bank, which was housed in the Bethesda Naval Medical Center, better known as the Navy Medical Center, across Wisconsin Avenue from the National Institutes of Health (NIH).

"The Navy Tissue Bank was really the beginning," said Helen Bottenfield, a critical care nurse who began work for the renal transplant program at Norfolk General Hospital in 1980 and then moved to the Virginia Tissue Bank, which later became LifeNet, in Virginia Beach, Virginia. "It was the genesis of modern-day tissue banking."

Early Technologies at the Navy Tissue Bank

In 1950, a year after the founding of the Navy Tissue Bank, injuries to military personnel fighting in the Korean War increased the demand for tissue—exactly the scenario Dr. Hyatt had envisioned when he proposed the program to Congress. "All these injured servicemen needed bone and soft tissue grafts," said Bottenfield. "Someone had to develop a way those critically needed grafts could be obtained, preserved, and sent to the front to treat those servicemen."

With this challenge on his mind, Dr. Hyatt embraced a technology he had learned in the 1930s from Dr. Earl Flosdorf, a biochemist at the University of Pennsylvania's School of Medicine, and to which Dr. Hyatt had been exposed during World War II. Dr. Flosdorf had been freeze-drying blood so the American Red Cross would have a reliable supply of plasma for treating American troops injured in battle overseas. Dr. Hyatt wanted to replicate this freezing process with bone, and he convinced the department chairman to purchase a small freezer for storing surplus bone collected from orthopedic surgical cases.[12] Subsequently, he realized freeze-drying to be a superior process, and brought in Flosdorf to collaborate in experiments on freeze-drying bones, skin, dura mater, arteries, and other human tissues necessary for the restoration of servicemen injured on

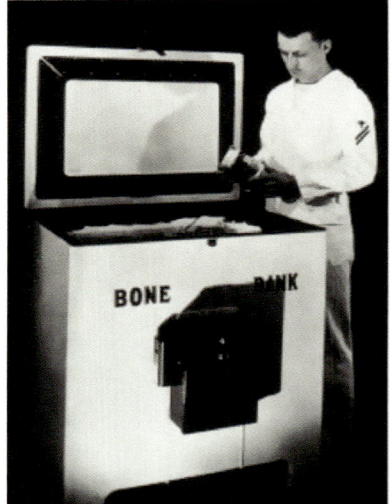

Navy Tissue Bank Freezer

Dr. George W. Hyatt
Father of American Tissue Banking

Dr. George W. Hyatt can be considered the father of American tissue banking. A combat veteran from South Dakota who studied medicine at Creighton University, Dr. Hyatt did not invent tissue banking, but he talked Congress into funding a tissue bank at the Naval Hospital in Bethesda, MD. This tissue bank then served as the incubator for many of tissue banking's leading practitioners, including Drs. Ted Melinin, Robert Stevenson, and Ken Sell, who of course went on to found the AATB.

Dr. Hyatt recruited physicians and researchers to the Navy Tissue Bank and conducted some of the earliest work on the use of frozen and freeze-dried skin and bone grafts on combat injuries. He served as the physician to Defense Department officials, orthopedic consultant to the White House physician's office, and chairman of the commission on emergency medical services of the American Medical Association. He also served as an international consultant to other tissue preservation programs as they were being founded.

Dr. Hyatt served for 17 years in the Navy before becoming a professor and, for much of his tenure, chairman of the division of orthopedic surgery at Georgetown University Medical Center. He won the Bronze Star and received the Navy League Award of Merit, the Exceptional Service Award of the U.S. Surgeon General, and the Bicentennial Medal of Georgetown University.

Dr. Hyatt died at age 63 in 1993.

the battlefield. The bones were deep-frozen with the use of liquid nitrogen which an engineer would produce and use as a coolant. Once the basic freeze-drying process was developed, Navy physicians conducted experiments to standardize preservation techniques for different tissues.

Dr. Robert Stevenson, a microbiologist and virologist and head of the Cell Tissue section at the National Institute of Health from 1958 to1960, noted that another of the pioneers in freeze-drying, Dr. Harold Meryman (AATB president, 1981– 83), was also at the Naval Medical Research Institute and was actively freeze-drying bone in concert with Dr. Hyatt. "He had a really comprehensive grasp of these things," said Dr. Robert Stevenson. "He preserved units of crushed bone and proposed that the Navy stockpile these for use by naval surgeons in the treatment of war wounds and other injuries, such as burns, that would occur in the normal circumstances of naval activities." Dr. Meryman's plan made sense, because freeze-dried tissue can be stored easily, safely, and reliably at room temperature, stockpiled in preparation for mass casualties, and easily reconstituted.

Additional Developments

The Navy Tissue Bank began as a bone bank, but it also stored some additional musculoskeletal tissues such as Achilles tendons. In 1950, Navy physicians developed a new method for preserving skin for up to 185 days by refrigerating it in a balanced saline solution. In May 1951, the Navy Tissue Bank opened a new surgical suite and performed the first recovery of tissue under aseptic conditions from a deceased donor.[13] The next year, in 1952, "the first clinical evaluations of arterial allografts were carried out with such success that the Navy requested all its hospitals to assist in the procurement of tissue."[14] And the following year, 1953, the donation and

CHAPTER ONE: A GROWING NEED: TISSUE BANKING, 1949–1976

retrieval of fascia lata and dura mater began.

These technologies successfully preserved tissues and bones so they could be sent anywhere in the world. After the Korean War, the Navy Tissue Bank continued to send tissue throughout its hospitals and medical centers around the world.

By that time, procurement of all human tissue required consent from the donor or, if the donor was deceased, from the family. The Navy Tissue Bank was the first U.S. bank to formalize the consent for donation process with a standardized form. Before the consent form was created, the standard practice was for a physician to ask the patient's family for donation of the bones and other muscu-loskeletal tissues. "If the donor's family agreed, tissue bank personnel would recover and process the tissue in an operating room right there at the tissue bank," stated Dr. Tomford. Soon, the Navy Tissue Bank was regularly storing—with consent—skin, bone, blood vessels, cartilage, and nerves.

In the late 1950s, during the brief peacetime after the Korean War and before casualties started returning to the U.S. from the Vietnam War, the Navy Tissue Bank distributed donated tissue to surgeons who were prepared to utilize them on an experimental basis in their practices.

By the early 1960s, the technology—at least as it related to blood—had spread to the private sector when Union Carbide, through its Linde

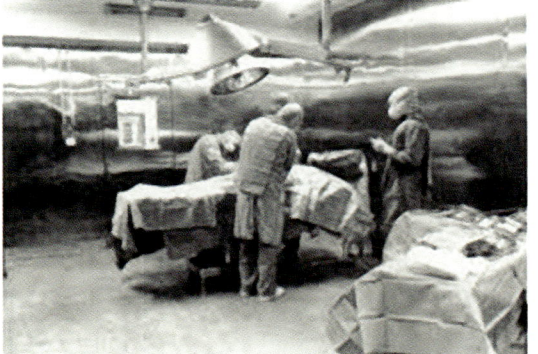

NTB Operating Theater

Division, developed automatic blood processing machines in which pint volumes of whole blood could be cooled and thawed rapidly.[15] Said Dr. Stevenson, who helped found the Society for Cryobiology in 1964, "It became possible to freeze tissues using protective agents. You could freeze tissue and actually have it come back to fully functioning capability." New uses for tissues were identified, and medical schools began to incorporate into their curricula training in procedures involving human tissue.

At the same time, the Navy Tissue Bank was called upon once again to support the troops. Casualties from Vietnam created such a high demand for donated tissue that additional recovery facilities were opened at the naval hospitals in San Diego and in Boston.

Establishment of Legal, Written Consent for Donation

Tissue banking expanded faster than the protocols, which led to confusion about what qualified as a legal donation. In 1961, the British Human Tissue Act was introduced to address the recovery of tissue from deceased donors. The act made it possible for people in Great Britain to consent or forbid donation after their death.

In the United States, multiple local statutes were enacted during the 1960s in response to cases brought by medical examiners and coroners concerning people who had died unexpectedly or in suspicious circumstances. Generally, the laws made organs, eyes, and tissues removed during an autopsy available for forensic investigation, but not for donation. Improperly procured tissue could easily lead to a lawsuit from the decedent's family.

In response to these varying legal statutes, The National Cancer Institute, which was responsible for setting up a resource program for cell banking and human tissues, hired an attorney to examine laws across the country related to the transport or procurement of human tissue. "Her report revealed many laws that made the transportation of human tissue across state lines illegal," said Dr. Stevenson, who noted that the revelations about the broad legal inconsistencies nationwide eventually led to the development of the Uniform Anatomical Gift Act (UAGA) of 1968, to which the National Research Institute subcommittee on transplantation (chaired by Dr. Stevenson) contributed.

The UAGA was a landmark in the history of organ, eye, and tissue donation. A donation statute, it was drafted during an era when civil rights were central in the national discourse, and the rights of the individual were being celebrated. This translated into the right of every citizen to do with his or her body as he or she saw fit. The UAGA codified this idea, giving the donor the first and also the decisive voice as long as their intentions were written and signed in the presence of two witnesses. As with the British Human Tissue Act of seven years earlier, written consent from the decedent superseded any rights of the next of kin. In cases where there was no written consent from the decedents themselves, UAGA granted next of kin the right to authorize or forbid a donation.

The Uniform Anatomical Gift Act was drafted by the National Conference of Commissioners on Uniform State Laws, providing a template for uniformity throughout the country. It also established the Uniform Donor Card as an official (although not legally enforceable) document of gift in all 50 states, identified the types and priority of individuals who could authorize donation, and enabled anyone over 18 to legally consent to donate.

By 1971, some form of the UAGA had been adopted in every state and the District of Columbia. The UAGA's exceptional popularity was stimulated by enthusiastic media coverage of recently improving rates of survival in kidney transplants, which had followed the discovery of powerful drugs for immunosuppression in the early 1960s. Before such drugs, the procedure had almost always been fatal, and had therefore ceased being performed. Once a favorable outcome became likely, the National Kidney Foundation successfully advocated for merging the donor card with the driver's license, which proved to be a major boon increasing both organ and tissue donation.

The Post-Vietnam Era

In 1965, after 17 years as director of the Navy Tissue Bank, Dr. George Hyatt left for a position at Georgetown University and was replaced by Dr. Kenneth W. Sell (AATB's first and fifth president), an immunopathologist who had already been at the Navy Tissue Bank for five years. Dr. Sell's arrival at the Navy Tissue Bank in 1960 was later deemed the start of "a new era in tissue bank history. Considered one of the pioneers in the field of transplantation and tissue banking, Sell brought expertise in immunology and cryobiology."[16] Dr. Sell remained as director until 1971, when he left to become chairman of the Department of Experimental and Clinical Immunology and commanding officer of the Naval Medical Research Institute (NMRI).

Dr. Sell was succeeded by Dr. Gary Friedlaender (AATB president, 1983–85), who, along with his successors, presided over an institution that was

Dr. Gary Friedlaender

evolving once again in response to America's changing military activities. As the gradual American withdrawal from Vietnam in the early 1970s resulted in fewer mass casualties, the previous need for large quantities of donated human tissue fell, and the Navy Tissue Bank turned its attention to organ and bone marrow transplantation. David Campagnari, a Navy tissue bank specialist in San Diego at the time, noted, "We were storing donations of bone marrow and ultimately stem cells. That was the beginning of a new program which eventually became the National Marrow Donor Program."

The field of tissue banking was maturing as it expanded beyond the Navy. Many professionals from the Navy Tissue Bank who retired from military service resumed their civilian careers and established small tissue banks at their local hospitals. Some, like the University of Miami Tissue Bank, begun by Navy Tissue Bank alumnus Dr. Ted Malinin, were affiliated with major medical centers. Others, like the Mile High Transplant Bank in Colorado, founded in 1982, and the Eastern Virginia Tissue Bank in Virginia Beach, founded by Bill Anderson in 1982, were developed as independent organizations, meaning they had no direct affiliation with or funding from a specific source such as a medical center or a university. These new tissue banks were "pretty locally focused in terms of not only procurement, but also distribution," said Jeff Sandler, an independent consultant and early employee at the Mile High Transplant Bank.

The NIH had a tissue procurement program, and some neurosurgeons and orthopedic surgeons stored allograft bones, and cardiologists stored donated aortas and valves, at their hospitals throughout the country in the early 1970s. There were also sperm banks and eye banks of varying degrees of formality. "All kinds of banking of

Bill Anderson

In Virginia Beach, in a first-floor hallway of LifeNet Health, the organ procurement organization for most of Virginia and the nation's largest full-service non-profit tissue and organ bank, there are various memorials from the families of organ and tissue donors. One of them, a quilt, honors Bill Anderson, one of the pioneers in the transplant field and the 1982 founder of the Eastern Virginia Tissue Bank, which became LifeNet.

Age 50 and CEO of LifeNet when he was killed in an auto accident in 2002, Anderson naturally became a donor. Of Anderson, Walter Graham, the executive director of the United Network for Organ Sharing (UNOS), said, "The first word that comes to mind is 'beloved.' He was highly regarded for his work, and he stood for compassion, excellence, and service."

Bill Anderson

A Wake Forest University biology graduate, Anderson was working in at Bowman Gray Hospital in Winston-Salem, North Carolina, when Sentara Norfolk General Hospital recruited him to come up to Norfolk. He ended up in organ procurement, "working with a lot of donors who served severely injured patients—trauma, gunshot wounds, aneurisms etc," said Doug Wilson, executive vice president of marketing at LifeNet. "The doctors at Sentara told Anderson that they were helping him get kidneys but they needed some bone for all spine procedures and didn't want to wait weeks. So that was the informal challenge to the local organ bank."

Anderson knew about the Navy Tissue Bank, which he called, and soon a team of corpsmen arrived via helicopter and recovered some tissue from a patient in the Sentara operating room. Over the next few months, teams came down from Bethesda to repeat the procedure, and Anderson and Helen Bottenfield, whom he had recruited to help him, would scrub in with them and learn how to do it themselves. By 1982, they had formed the Eastern Virginia Tissue Bank, a one-room facility in a strip mall.

Today, 35 years later, LifeNet Health has nearly 900 employees, including four full-time and two part-time medical directors.

human tissue was taking place," said Dr. Stevenson.

These facilities fell outside any existing framework regulating licensed medical practitioners, pharmaceuticals, biologicals, and medical consumables. While the UAGA regulated donation, tissue-banking practices could vary. There were no commonly accepted rules or guidelines, and no recommended procedures or protocols relating to processing, storing, and distribution. As a result, professionals like Drs. Sell, Friedlaender, and Stevenson grew concerned about the possibility of unsafe practices.

One incipient regional association, the Southeastern Organ Procurement Foundation, attempted to step in and provide some organization and support, but it failed to gain traction. Another loose confederation called the Western Association of Tissue Banks, which hosted about a dozen small regional tissue banks in a gathering once a quarter, was more successful, but purely regional.

There was a need for a national body to provide organization, promote best practices, and establish widely recognized standards and protocols.

Elijah and Walker McGinley

Twenty weeks into her pregnancy, Jodie McGinley and her husband Jesse learned that she was carrying twin boys. Then they received the bad news. "During the ultrasound," said Jodie, "the tech put the probe back up on the machine, put his hand on my knee and said, 'We need to talk.' I felt like my world had stopped."

The doctor informed the McGinleys that baby A, Walker, looked fine, but that baby B, Elijah, appeared to have a neural tube defect called spina bifida, which causes paralysis of the lower extremities. "We knew we were going to have a challenge of two opposite twins, but we were prepared for it." said Jodie.

The McGinley and Gadbois-Cates families gather together around a picture of neonate donor Eli McGinley, whose aortic heart valve was donated to Cambrie Gadbois-Cates, right.

Jodie and Jesse began to pray in earnest for the baby they had come to call Eli. On August 3, 2009, at 36 weeks, Jesse and Jodie Walker (5 lbs, 7 oz) and Eli (6 lbs, 3 oz) into their lives. Their world turned upside down days later, however, when they learned that Eli's condition was much more severe than initially thought. "We immediately knew what we had to do." Jesse stated. "We had to give another baby the opportunity at life, another family the chance to keep their baby in their arms."

On August 6th at Arkansas Children's Hospital, three days after his birth, Eli was taken off life support while surrounded by his family. Expecting to have mere minutes with him, his parents and doctors were surprised when he continued breathing on his own.

A day later, in Eli's final hours of life at The University of Arkansas for Medical Sciences, the medical teams brought the twin brothers together for the last time. "It seemed almost like Eli was holding on to something, and it became obvious that that something was one last chance to be

Elijah and Walker McGinley

with his brother." Once the twins were reunited in Walker's NICU room, Eli's color returned to his little body and when his little hand was laid on top of his brother's shoulder, a smile, preserved in photographs, spread across his face. "The power of twins is incredible," says Jesse.

On August 8, 2009, in the arms of his parents and beside his twin brother, Eli took his last breath. That day, he gave the gift of life so that another child would be able to carry on, grow, and become healthy again. "We prayed over the babies that he would potentially save that night," says Jodie. "I also prayed and asked Eli to come back to me. It wasn't that I wanted him to come back to this life, but I just wanted sound confidence that we made the right decision with his life.

"Eli will always be perfect in our eyes. We gave birth to a hero. And we will continue to raise Walker to know his twin brother in everything we do in his life," says Jodie.

Five years after he passed, Eli was a 2014 Tournament of Roses "Donate Life Rose Parade Float" honoree. He was among 72 donors honored on the float that January 1st in Pasadena, California. About the same time, Jodie learned her prayers had been answered when the family received a call from CryoLife, of Kennesaw, Georgia, informing them that Eli's aortic heart valve had been transplanted into a two-day baby girl in Maine earlier that year, and that the little girl was thriving. In March, the McGinley's were able to fly out and meet Eli's valve recipient, Cambrie Gadbois-Cates. "She was the most beautiful little dark-haired girl I had ever laid eyes on," says Jodie. "It was like a dream to know she was carrying our little man in that tiny little chest." The McGinley family and the Gadbois-Cates family have continued their close friendship and have been privileged to travel the U.S. together in sharing their neonatal donor-recipient experience.

Two years later, CryoLife informed the McGinleys that Eli's pulmonary valve had been sent on a Doctors Without Borders (through CryoKids) trip to the Dominican Republic for transplant. The recipient, 9-year-old Luis Angel Mercado, received Eli's pulmonary valve as a two-cusp onlay patch on April 15, 2016.

From Arkansas to Maine and the Domincan Republic, Eli's gift of life has enabled him to travel the world one life at a time.

Dr. Kenneth Sell

Chapter Two:
Setting the Standards: The Early Years of the AATB, 1976–1987

"The AATB began with the thought that it would be helpful to have an association of tissue banks," said Dr. William Tomford. "Ken Sell's original idea was that there were issues involving tissue procurement, tissue storage, and tissue sterilization, and the banks in the U.S. could meet and discuss how each bank performed these procedures."

Such an association was more than a good idea; it was quickly becoming a necessity. Although many practitioners had benefited from the Navy's experience, the time had come to organize a professional association to promote exchange of information, methods, and procedures; increase the number of donations; establish a code of ethics; and address the medical and legal implications of transplantation. Looking ahead, the leaders in the field recognized that at some point the government would begin to draft regulations for tissue banking unless the tissue-banking community itself was proactive in reaching and then expressing peer consensus on standards and procedures.

In August of 1975, Dr. Ken Sell convened a meeting in Washington, D.C. of 50 to 100 clinicians and researchers from around the country who were using transplantable banked human tissue. The American Association of Tissue Banks was subsequently incorporated in Maryland in June of 1976. "Encouraging best practices and defining problems that needed attention were the driving forces at the beginning," said Dr. Stevenson.

"I think Ken Sell also had the concept of individual memberships," said Dr. Tomford. "This approach provided the organization with a small financial basis in the early years. There were only a few banks at that time, so the organization could not rely on dues from these banks for sufficient support. The Navy Tissue Bank had maybe 15 or 20 people assigned [to the AATB meeting]. The Miami Tissue Bank directed by Dr. Ted Malinin and Dr. Donald Prolo, a neurosurgeon who founded a bank in California, helped start the association."

"The idea," said Dr. Robert Stevenson, another driving force and a presenter at the meeting, "was that if you became a member of the AATB, you were also encouraged to join an AATB council, which was tissue-oriented. We had skin, bone, eye, cell… a variety of areas, so that during our meetings, people who were active in those particular fields could hear speakers and subjects that were of current or topical interest specifically to them. For the general meetings we would give presentations on general topics such as cryopreservation, or include general topics of medical legal issues, which would be of interest to all of the members."

For instance, one of the first speakers was Dr. Julie Glowacki, a biological chemist who spoke on bone proteins.

Dr. Sell was elected by the founding members as the director and first president. Other officers were Vernon P. Perry, director and vice chair; John C. Sasso, director and treasurer; James E. Ostrander, director and secretary; and Monroe M. Vincent, director. The early councils were musculoskeletal, reproductive, skin, and tissue bank, the latter of which incorporated a variety of tissue-related subjects.

Dr. Michael Joyce, (AATB president, 1989-99), a young orthopedic surgeon at the Cleveland Clinic, immediately recognized the benefit of sharing information. "If you had an interest in something and the standards in your field applied to my issues, we could work through it together to find mutual-

CHAPTER TWO: SETTING THE STANDARDS: THE EARLY YEARS OF THE AATB, 1976–1987

Table of Organization
American Association of Tissue Banks

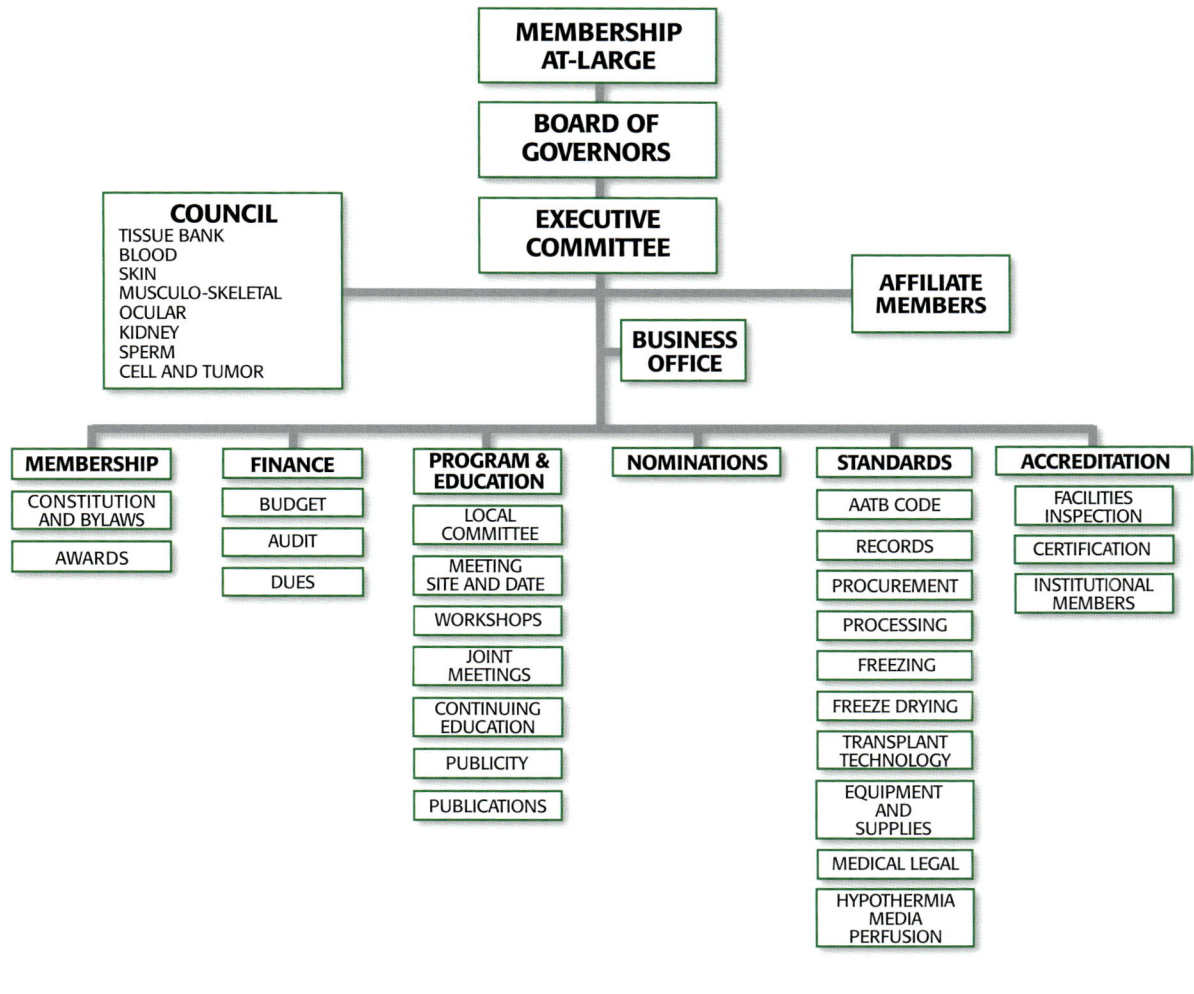

Tissue Bank Symposium

August 13–15, 1975
Washington, D.C.

Organizers

Kenneth W. Sell, M.D., Ph.D.
Captain, Medical Corps, U.S. Navy
Commanding Officer, Naval Medical Research Institute
Bethesda, Maryland
and
American Institute of Biological Sciences
Arlington, Virginia

Program Committee

Kenneth W. Sell, M.D., Ph.D., *Chairman*
Captain, Medical Corps, U.S. Navy
Gary E. Friedlaender, M.D.
Lieutenant Commander, Medical Corps, U.s. Naval Reserve
Vernon P. Perry
Lieutenant Commander, Medical Service Corps, U.S. Navy (Retired)
James E. Ostrander, *Secretary*
Betty J. Sylvester, *Editorial Staff*
Janie P. Kaczmarowski, *Editorial Staff*

Welcoming Remarks
C.E. Brodine
Captain, Medical Corps, U.S. Navy

It is indeed a pleasure to welcome such a distinguished group of scientists to the Tissue Bank Symposium. This symposium is particularly significant to those of us in the Navy, since 1975 marks the 25th anniversary of the organization of the Navy Tissue Bank at Bethesda. The program speakers and the wide spectrum of subjects are evidence of the scope and the quality that this meeting promises.

Transplantation of nonviable grafts, such as bone, was not successfully accomplished between humans until the late 19th century. Until more recently, patients with diseased or nonfunctioning organs either survived their illnesses or died. The problems related to transplantation of viable organs, including surgical technique, tissue typing, and the successful management of graft rejection, seemed insurmountable until well after the turn of the century.

Progress in tissue and organ transplantation research intensified in the 1930s and led to developments responsible for subsequent clinical success. The advent of the artificial kidney, for example, enabled patients with end-stage renal disease to survive until a suitable donor could be identified. Tissue-typing procedures and experience with immunosuppressive therapy appropriate for abrogating problems related to allograft replacement have greatly improved the efficacy of organ transplantation.

The first successful transplant of human bone marrow occurred in 1939, and the first successful human renal transplant was accomplished in 1954. Since then, liver, lung, pancreas, and heart have joined the list of approximately 25 types of tissues and organs that have demonstrated successful clinical application.[1] Kidneys are the most frequently transplanted viable organ, having increased in the United States from 428 in 1967 to 1,529 in 1971.[2]

Another important development relates to facilities. Today we recognize that there are several types of tissue-bank facilities in the world. There are those that process and store all forms of tissues and make them available to transplant surgeons worldwide. There are also tissue banks that specialize in specific tissues and organs, such as bone and corneas. There are, in addition, facilities that are not really banks but reference and collection centers that provide tissues within a particular region.

This meeting will address all three types of facilities and provide a description of the full spectrum of tissue-banking techniques available in the reparative surgical field. As the individual responsible for the management of the Navy Medical Department's research and development programs, I hope that you will find time during your discussions to identify those problems that require attention and emphasis by the research community.

REFERENCES:
1. American Medical Association Committee on Transfusion and Transplantation: Donation of Bodies or Organs for Transplantation and Medical Sciences. Chicago, AMA, 1974

2. Isler C: RN 35:36-43 (Nov), 1972

ly acceptable practices, also taking into account the safety of the tissue, etc."

"It was an association of people who shared a common language," said Dr. Ross Wilkins, an orthopedic surgeon with the Mayo Clinic who would later relocate to Denver to work with the Mile High Transplant Bank, now known as AlloSource.

Those types of discussions immediately paved the way for the guidelines the Association set out to establish as a foundation for publishing formal standards. Between 1978 and 1981, discussions encompassed specific cells and tissues divided into renal, ocular, cell, and tumor tissues; bone marrow; musculoskeletal; semen; and skin. The first draft of the *Guidelines for Tissue Banking* was published in 1977. After revisions were made over the years, the tissue-specific portion of these guidelines resulted in the AATB *Technical Manual*. As the AATB had no formal power to sanction any of its members, the standards were voluntary, and each tissue bank could choose whether or not to adhere to them.

AATB President Dr. Harold Meryman recognized that the AATB needed a full-time executive director, and in July of 1983, Jeanne Mowe, then the manager of the public information office of the research center at the National Cancer Institute at Frederick, was hired. That same year, the AATB moved from their original offices in Rockville, Maryland, to larger accommodations in Arlington, Virginia.

In 1984, the *AATB Standards for Tissue Banking* were published in the first of what are now 14 increasingly expanded editions (although they were not called "editions" until the 10th revision). This collection marked the first professional standards ever developed in the field of banking transplantable human tissues, other than ocular, and it came with the following encomium:

These general Standards are intended to be applicable to any and all forms of tissue banking: retrieval, storage, and distribution of human tissues for medical use. They represent the current thinking of a diversified group of experienced practitioners of tissue banking who have pooled their efforts to extract general principles and philosophies of banking operations common to all and to highlight specific considerations which pertain to certain categories of tissues."

A lot of work went on outside official AATB gatherings. For instance, Dr. Michael Joyce pointed out that "people felt there was a need for guidelines on how to fulfill the standards," so, "in the mid-1980s, 15 of us convened at Massachussets General Hospital for a three-day weekend and worked trying to establish additional standards and also guidelines, especially for musculoskeletal tissue." Extracurricular work of this nature would be incorporated at annual meetings and in the next publication of the *Standards*.

AATB and Tissue-Banking Culture

In the early years, the AATB was a small and fairly close-knit group of specialists from around the country. "The AATB provided a nice forum for a bunch of us who had the same interests to get together and share ideas," said Glenn Greenleaf, who then worked recovering tissue in the burn center at UC San Diego, and who has served as director of tissue service operations at LifeCell since 1994.

Helen Bottenfield, who had just started working for Bill Anderson at the Eastern Virginia Tissue Bank in Virginia Beach, recalled attending her first meeting around 1984. "It was so much fun every year to be a part of AATB because it was growing and changing as new people became involved. There were probably less than 100 people in the meeting room! If you attend an AATB meeting now, there will be at least 800 to 900 attendees.

"Some people viewed those of us involved primarily in organ procurement with a little bit of suspicion," she continued. "There really had never been any concentration on combining organ and tissue donation at the point of donation. It became abundantly clear from the initial evaluation and authorization that donation is donation, regardless of the organ, tissue, or eyes to be recovered. The donor's family and the donor—the way you treated them—was the same regardless of the type of donation, no matter what. It was inevitable that these two important areas of transplantation would come together."

David Campagnari joined the AATB in the early 1980s, like Bottenfield and Greenleaf. "There were a number of organizations that were looking to get involved in tissue banking at that particular time," he said. "Jeanne Mowe, who was the executive director of AATB, actually introduced me to others so I could meet a number of people who were looking to start tissue programs."

Dr. Richard Kagan (AATB president, 1999–2001), a general surgeon who specialized in burn care, was especially interested in skin donation.

"The hospital where I worked in Chicago thought it would be beneficial to our patients to have a skin bank, so I became involved in skin banking and joined the AATB." In the early 1980s, he was one of the early members from outside the musculoskeletal field. "I learned a great deal from people like Dr. Randy May who had been banking human skin for many years," he recalled.

Education and Training

Early on, it became clear that a standardized program of education had to be provided for those entering the field, so continuing education for its members was an early AATB priority. In the early 1980s, the AATB began its education and training with workshops on musculoskeletal and skin banking and tissue transplantation. "Our commitment to maintaining the public's trust was a major factor in moving this initiative forward," said Bottenfield. "Formal training courses for people that were new to tissue banking were planned and executed by leaders from the tissue-banking profession."

About the same time, there was a move to develop standard education for all aspects of tissue banking to ensure that the safety bar was always set to the highest level. An education committee was formed and charged by AATB President Dr. William Tomford to take on the task of planning formal training courses and beginning the work of developing formal testing and certification of tissue bank technicians. "The AATB was devoted to education and improving the baseline for the industry," said cryotechnologist Russ Bierbaum of ReproTech, a reproductive tissue bank with multiple locations across the country.

Early Procurement and Screening

Public awareness about donation was increasing due to a focused effort on public education as a collaboration of donation agencies and the health resources and service administration of the Department of Health and Human Services. Bottenfield's experience in her own Virginia region was typical. "It was a natural evolution to add tissue donation to the services we already provided for organ donation, and in many cases it provided options for donation to families that had never been available in the past. Our local hospital professionals were both receptive and helpful in facilitation of tissue donation as a value-added service both to the donor and, ultimately, for recipients.

"I also give the public a lot of credit," she said, "because there were a lot of families who really pushed the issue." One new widower, she stated, insisted on donating his wife's organs and tissues because, "she wanted to help as many people as she could."

Slowly, more and more organizations developed their own principles and guidelines related to tissue banking. A subcategory of "living donor" surgical bone banking helped pave the way to better screening techniques for all donations. "During the time before regulations, hospitals would save femoral heads removed during hip revisions and put them in a large jar of iodine or other solution where they would just sit until a doctor needed some bone for another case," said Diane Wilson (AATB president, 2009–11). "There were a couple of cases of transmission of hepatitis B, though, after which they began to take measure to improve safety by processing these femoral heads separately, and retesting the living donors six months after the donation."

It soon became apparent that additional screening was required for both living and deceased donors, so, as Dr. Michael Joyce noted, "We started tests for syphilis and then hepatitis B. At that time, in the early 1980s, testing had not begun for either HIV or hepatitis C."

Establishment of the National Organ Transplant Act

The UAGA had codified the right of individuals to determine what transpired with their tissues and organs after death, but this legislation did not address the legal issues involving tissue procured without consent or tissue imported from other countries. Fifteen years after the provision of the UAGA, Senators Al Gore and Orrin Hatch introduced a bill seeking to support and define some legal parameters around organ transplantation, and began committee hearings at which Drs. Sell and Stevenson both testified. In February of 1984, Dr. Stevenson, at the time chair of the AATB *Standards* Committee, sought to educate the panel about the importance of including tissue, in addition to organs, in the legislation. "While prospective donors may elect which tissues will be donated through the donor card mechanism and next-of-kin permission, their wishes may often be frustrated because the funding, the facility, and the staff are oriented toward solid organ procurement only. It is the belief of our Association that federal support should also be available to full-service tissue banks that will serve a broad medical need."

These arguments prevailed and tissue was soon included in the organ donation discussion. Though outside the strict purview of its responsibilities, because of these kinds of contributions, the AATB was appointed to the National Task Force on Organ Transplantation. Such collaboration would become the rule rather than the exception for the AATB. For instance, the AATB also assisted the American Association of Blood Banks in setting standards.

On October 19, 1984, President Ronald Reagan signed the Gore Bill, as it was known colloquially, into law as the National Organ Transplantation Act (NOTA), which outlawed the sale of human organs and tissue. NOTA isolated the pool of available organs and tissues to those that had a provenance of donation and had subsequently gone through appropriate steps. In other words, a prospective recipient could rest easier knowing that, barring those procured by an unethical physician, any allograft organ or tissue was not coming from the black market.

NOTA went beyond lawmaking to regulation by creating the Task Force on Organ Transplantation. Under the umbrella of the Department of Health and Human Services, the task force was authorized to allocate $2 million annually toward the operation of organ procurement organizations, or OPOs, around the country, all of which would be linked by the Organ Procurement and Transplantation Network,[17] "a public-private partnership that links all professionals involved in the U.S. donation and transplantation system [including] individuals who sign organ donor cards, people who comment on policy proposals and countless volunteers who support donation and transplantation, among many others."[18]

"It was all going to be guided by federal rules and regulations," said Dan Shires, executive vice president of LifeLink, a tissue bank in Tampa. "They divied up the service areas."

"The OPOs were regulated monopolies," agreed Sue Dunn, president and CEO of Donor Alliance, an OPO in Colorado and Wyoming.

The network helped ensure that physicians—and ultimately patients—who need organs or tissues for transplant would have nationwide, instead of merely local, access to donations. OPOs like Donor Alliance operate on the local or regional level, registering donors, running campaigns to increase the pool of available donors, and actually coordinating the donation process, taking the administrative burden off physicians and hospitals who had until this time usually donated their time to build local banks.

Consolidation of the donation process under OPOs also ensured grieving families would not face multiple inquiries seeking donations of corneas, organs, and tissues. OPOs reduced the donation process to one channel and one conversation, and thereby minimized the potential for stress on donor families and hospital staff.

Such legal and professional advances came none too soon, because in the early 1980s a human immunodeficiency virus (HIV) epidemic began in the United States. "That was a major game changer," said Dr. Michael Joyce. "We were concerned about HIV, but we also realized that there were other viruses." The HIV screening test became available in 1985, and consequently the Public Health Service, a division of the United States Department of Health and Human Services that safeguards and promotes public health through professionals placed in numerous government departments and agencies, recommended testing for HIV all potential donors of blood, plasma, organs, tissues, and/or semen.

Patient First! The Establishment of the Inspection Program and the Accreditation Committee

If there was a theme to all the increasing activities in which the AATB engaged, and all the initiatives it supported, during the 1980s, it would have been "patient first." All the efforts to ensure quality, uniformity, safety, research, and the adoption of best practices worked toward that one goal.

Anticipating regulation by the FDA, the AATB sought to proactively harmonize how the profession approached the processing of tissues. Practically speaking, this meant that AATB member banks sought to demonstrate to physicians that all tissue banks were abiding by the same standards, if not the exact same procedures. The idea was that physicians would know a tissue bank that was a member of the AATB would be following carefully reviewed safety guidelines.

"I think that was the strength of the AATB," said Greenleaf, "the foresight of the people who put this together and who wanted to harmonize this approach to assure clinicians that the tissue they were getting from one bank was the same as the tissue they were getting from another bank."

The AATB attempted to encourage this consistency of practice through a peer review inspection program that began in 1985. "In the early years," said Dr. Joyce, "two of us would go down and inspect someone else's bank and make some constructive suggestions. The only cost of this was the travel expenses related to flying us there."

To further encourage tissue banks to adhere to standards, the AATB established a voluntary accreditation program in 1986, which made compliance with the *Standards* mandatory for accreditation. At that point, said David Campagnari, "individual banks still had to decide whether or not it was worth the effort, or of any value, to become an AATB-accredited tissue bank. There were quite a few banks that chose not to participate because they did not see the value of the AATB accreditation, or the need to follow the standards. For quite a few years, it seemed like there were only 10 to 12 tissue banks that were accredited."

Over the next decade, the AATB would not only revise standards, but also enhance its education and training programs, outsource inspections, and establish a professional relationship with the FDA. In the process, the AATB became widely recognized as the authority in the field.

A Tale of Two Athletes

Growing up, Mike Erickson played football and enjoyed the outdoors. He was very quick-witted, with an exceptional sense of humor. His mother Dorothy describes him as a computer geek, and says he had talked about going to school in the computer field. Before graduation, Mike enlisted in the Marine Corps.

Tragically, Mike passed away at the age of 28. He donated his tissues, organs, and corneas, helping more than 100 people through his gift.

"When I got the word that he was in the ER, I headed out immediately," Dorothy said. "My mind was full of Mike and his life, which was ending way too soon. I knew before I arrived at the hospital that if it were an option, Mike would have wanted to help others one last time. That's why I made the decision to donate."

About the same time Mike passed away, a young man named Colin, a high school junior, injured his knee sliding into second base while playing baseball. One morning, Colin could not get out of bed because his knee had locked and he could not bend it. He visited his doctor, and within four days, he was in surgery.

Colin's doctor told him that he could repair his knee by removing 50 percent of the weight bearing in that knee. The surgeon would need to perform an allograft transplant to replace what he was removing.

Mike Erickson's meniscus was used to repair Colin's knee. "Thanks to my donor [Mike], I will be able to function normally in my daily life and live without the pain it was causing me," Colin said. Colin also says that he plans on being a donor himself, which is something he had never thought of before he "realized how special it is to receive a gift that is so important."

Mike's parents exchanged letters with Colin, who expressed his deep sense of gratitude for the gift of tissue donation. Dorothy expressed that she had been hoping and praying that the recipients of Mike's gifts had been getting stronger and resuming normal lives, and receiving Colin's letter helped to answer that question. As a result of experiences like this, Dorothy believes in the gift of life, and has become an advocate for it. "Because of, or in spite of, our losses, many others will have the opportunity to have better lives. We can't do better than that."

"If you were wondering what kind of individual Mike was," she says, "he was kind-hearted and quiet. I know he would be very happy to know that part of him lives on in you," wrote Dorothy.

Mike was honored for his gift of tissue donation through a florograph of Mike that adorned the 2015 "Donate Life Rose Parade Float" on January 1, 2015, in Pasadena, California.

Jeanne Mowe

Chapter Three:
Challenges, Collaboration, and Contractors: Taking the Next Step, 1987–2000

The late 1980s and early 1990s brought a plethora of changes and challenges on administrative, public health, and regulatory fronts, but the most obvious change was in the dynamic growth of the tissue-banking community.

The Growth of the Tissue-Banking Profession and the Inception of Large Tissue Banks

Because it was a burgeoning new area of medical activity, careers in tissue banking were beginning almost by accident. "I don't think anybody back in the day expected tissue banking would have been a career," said Greenleaf. "It's different today because the field is pretty well established."

Some of today's largest processors had modest beginnings (as described immediately below) in the 1980s and 1990s, several of them under different names than they have today. In alphabetical order, Acelity/LifeCell, AlloSource, Community Tissue Services (CTS), CryoLife, LifeLink Tissue Bank, LifeNet Health, MiMedx, Musculoskeletal Transplant Foundation (MTF), RTI Surgical/RTI Donor Services, and University of Miami Tissue Bank (UMTB) represent the majority of the organizations that would shape tissue banking 20 and 30 years after their founding. All but MiMedx were founded before 2000.

Acelity (Formerly LifeCell)

LifeCell began in the early 1980s as a private venture technology transfer from the University of Texas when two researchers, Dr. John Linner and Dr.

Stephen Livesey, developed cryobiological technology that dramatically improved cell preservation.

Located in The Woodlands, Texas, LifeCell initially focused on tissue and blood cell preservation, receiving grants from the U.S. Department of Defense to continue development on a method to preserve and store human blood at room temperature for extended periods. In the early 1990s, LifeCell began applying unique tissue preservation technologies to donated tissue. In 1994, the first transplant of its acellular dermal matrix was performed.

AlloSource

In 1982, members of the Junior League of Denver raised $130,000 to establish both a Mothers' Milk Bank and the Mile High Transplant Bank, which was designed to be a full-service transplant bank serving the Rocky Mountain region. In the early 1990s, "some Organ Procurement Organizations (OPOs) were looking around to see who to work with," said AlloSource founder, Senior Medical Director and orthopedic surgeon Dr. Ross Wilkins. "Our methods, techniques, and standards in Denver worked well, so a few of us, including orthopedic oncologist Dr. Steve Gitelis [who was working with the Organ Bank of Illinois at Chicago's Rush University Medical Center], decided to pool our resources." The new organization, created by three OPO Corporate Members, became AlloSource, with a mission to honor the gift of tissue donation by maximizing its medical impact.

Community Tissue Services (CTS)

In 1988, open-heart surgery nurse Diane Wilson became the director of the Dayton Regional Tissue Bank. "Dayton Regional was a little, tiny tissue bank," said Wilson, "but we did it all: recovered, processed, and distributed tissue." Despite its size, Dayton Regional strived to become a leader in the area. "Once we started to grow, we found the need to change our name to Community Tissue Services," said Wilson.

CryoLife, Inc.

"In 1984, CryoLife was a small, start-up biomedical company," said Jeff Wiggins, who was the nineteenth employee at the company and now is senior manager of training and education of the donor services department. "We were housed in a 2,400-square-foot laboratory near Hartsfield Airport in southwest Atlanta." CryoLife specialized in the low temperature preservation of cardiovascular tissue. The company grew quickly as the leading cardiovascular tissue processor in the 1980s and, in the 1990s, developed a decellularization technology that reduced panel reactive antibodies (PRA) by removing allogeneic donor cells but maintained the structural integrity of the tissue matrix. CryoLife also acquired the initial patents and technology for a surgical adhesive that would eventually be used worldwide.

LifeLink Tissue Bank

Established in 1985 as the Florida Regional Bone and Tissue Bank, LifeLink worked closely with Dr. Ted Malinin from the University of Miami as strictly a recovery agency until 1989, when it completed the build out of the original tissue bank. The organization began processing its own donors in September of that year.

LifeNet Health

In 1975, recent Wake Forest graduate Bill Anderson began work in organ procurement at Bowman Gray Hospital in Winston-Salem, North Carolina. A few years later, he was recruited by Norfolk General Hospital to perform similar services there. In 1982, he started the Eastern Virginia Tissue Bank (EVTB), a small independent facility in a strip office building in Virginia Beach. As it grew, EVTB changed its name to the Virginia Tissue Bank (VTB) then, in 1989, to LifeNet Transplant Services. In 2000, LifeNet merged with Virginia's

Organ Procurement Organization (VOPA) to become the OPO for the majority of the Commonwealth of Virginia.

Musculoskeletal Transplant Foundation (MTF)

The Musculoskeletal Transplant Foundation, or MTF, was started in 1987 by seven leading orthopedic academic centers from around the country. For the first ten years of its life, all of the tissue recovered by or for MTF was processed by Osteotech. By 1998, MTF began processing specialized spine tissues on its own, eventually moving to the processing of all its own tissues. "MTF was an example of the non-profit model established with people who were interested in doing recoveries or setting up and using tissue banks," said former AATB President Dr. Michael Joyce. "MTF was built on the back of some academic centers in various cities."

RTI Surgical, Inc.

The University of Florida Tissue Bank (UFTB) was formed in 1982 as a non-profit to recover, process, and distribute tissue for transplantation. In 1998, via a technology transfer of its allograft processing operations, related equipment and technologies, distribution arrangements, and research and development activities, it became one of the first non-profit tissue banks to become for-profit as Regeneration Technologies in Alachua, Florida.

University of Miami Tissue Bank (UMTB)

The University of Miami Tissue Bank (UMTB) was founded in 1970 by Dr. Theodore I. Malinin, who received training and gained experience in tissue banking at the U.S. Navy Tissue Bank Naval Medical Research Institute. Originally housed in a three-room operating room suite and an office, the UMTB eventually acquired a 13,000-square-foot space with a dedicated O.R. suite for procurement, several aseptic processing rooms, and other facilities used for the storage and preparation of human tissue allografts under optimal conditions. By the 1990s, the University of Miami Tissue Bank, one of the few located inside an academic institution, was not only one of the oldest but one of the largest and most respected tissue banks in the country.

Administrative Changes

In 1991, the tissue banking community was mindful that science and technology would create new capabilities in transplantation, and that the profession would continue to grow. Wth change—like the emergence of large tissue banks—inevitable, the leadership of the AATB felt it was time to plan aggressively for the future.

In October of 1991, at the AATB's 15th annual meeting in Clearwater, Florida, the AATB, under the leadership of President Dr. Charles Cuono, a plastic surgeon, began its first strategic planning process with the formation of a steering committee and the selection of an outside planning firm. Early the next year, questionnaires were sent to members and outside organizations soliciting opinions about the AATB's mission, goals, strengths, weaknesses, and priorities, as well as about industry trends.

The Year 2000 Plan was presented at the annual meeting in 1992. It began with a mission statement:

As a leader in tissue and cell banking, the mission of the American Association of Tissue Banks is to establish and promulgate standards and foster education and research in banking to ensure quality and safety of tissues and cells for transplantation.

The plan then listed four goals, what are called the "brush strokes" of the plan:

1. Support tissue and cell banks
2. Ensure availability of safe, high quality tissues and cells for the public good

3. Advance AATB's position as a leader in tissue and cell banking
4. Strengthen the Association

These goals were supported by five objectives, each with a set of strategies to ensure success:

- Objective 1: Provide Leadership for Educational Programs in Tissue and Cell Banking Nationwide
- Objective 2: Develop and Promulgate the Highest Technical and Ethical Standards for Tissue and Cell Banking
- Objective 3: Foster Collaboration with Groups and Organizations with an Interest in Tissue and Cell Banking
- Objective 4: Promote Research in the Science of Tissue and Cell Banking and Transplantation Strategies

A task force was established to pursue the additional funding necessary to meet the mission and goals.

The same year Plan 2000 was presented, 1992, the AATB established the Medical Advisory Committee, to address clinical issues related to tissue banking, and the Governmental Affairs Committee, because the AATB and its members were becoming increasingly involved with governmental and legislative bodies. For example, members were testifying before the Senate Labor and Human Resources Committee on human tissue legislation, and the association as a whole was working more closely with the FDA, which was preparing to establish regulatory authority over tissue banking. Emphasizing this focus on both legislative and administrative matters, in 1993 the AATB published the first issue of *Tissue and Cell Report*, a journal that ran for about four years. That first edition, edited by AATB President

Dr. Ted Eastlund, addressed the role of chief executive officer in interacting with congressional agencies and with directors and managers of individual banks.

In 1993, the professionals who were primarily interested in cornea donation broke away from the AATB, and consequently the AATB abolished the Ocular Council. On the other hand, it established the Accredited Tissue Bank Council, or ATBC, designed as a forum for members to discuss issues solely related to tissue banks. Two members from this council were to be designated to serve on the Board of Governors.

The American Red Cross

Both the AATB's increasing focus on accreditation, begun in 1986, and its development of a comprehensive strategic plan, begun in 1991, occurred in the wake of a surprising external challenge from an unexpected faction. Throughout the mid-1980s, the American Red Cross, the largest blood organization on the world, had been dabbling in tissue banking at various chapters, most notably in the Midwest and New York State. A few of these Red Cross tissue banks also processed 100,000 allografts annually, largely musculoskeletal, from over 2,000 donors.[19]

At the AATB annual meeting in 1988, Red Cross CEO Bill Miller made a presentation announcing that the American Red Cross had decided to reorganize and consolidate its tissue-banking functions to become a major player in tissue banking. The Red Cross would procure tissue from 13 locations

Dr. Ted Eastlund

around the country and outsource the tissue processing to a private, new, for-profit company called Osteotech, which had been founded in 1986 and was based in New Jersey. Osteotech would then send the processed tissue back to the American Red Cross for distribution.

A nationwide tissue bank with a for-profit processor created some tensions within the field, but the reality was that there were simply too many tissue banks at the time for the American Red Cross to be as dominant as it had perhaps envisioned. In January of 2005, the American Red Cross sold the tissue-banking services to MTF in order to focus on its traditional core business: blood services and disaster relief.

Infectious Disease Challenges

HIV had been identified in the early 1980s, and the FDA developed donor-screening measures in 1985, but the period of time between one's exposure to HIV and the time that a blood test would register positive for the virus was problematic for these new screening measures. "Back in those days," said Dr. Rich Kagan, "there was about a 90-day window where you could have exposure, become infected, but test negative." In addition, family members who completed the medical/social history interview were often not aware of a potential donor's high-risk behavior. Similar to blood donation, "a donor at risk could slip through," said Dr. Kagan.

As a result, the AATB and other organizations began to focus more intently on determining risk factors to be used in donor screening and required testing when an HIV test became available. A working group formed by the Public Health Service (PHS) in 1991 to address these issues concluded that further recommendations should be made to reduce the already low risk of HIV transmission by transplantation of organs and tissues. The revised guidelines addressed issues such as donor screening, testing, and exclusionary criteria; quarantine of tissue from living donors; inactivation or elimination of infectious organisms in organs and tissues before transplantation; timely detection, reporting, and tracking of potentially infected tissues, organs, and recipients; and recall of stored tissues from donors found after donation to have been infected. The resultant *Comprehensive Guidelines for Prevention of HIV Transmission from Transplanted Organs and Tissues*,[20] completed in 1994, stipulated that the quarantine period for living donors would be doubled from 90 to 180 days. Contributing from the AATB or its membership to setting these new requirements were—among many others—Dr. Kenneth W. Sell; Dr. Charles B. Cuono; Dr. Scott Bottenfield, of Chicago; Dr. Richard L. Hurwitz, from LifeNet Transplant Services; Joel Osborne from Musculoskeletal Transplant Foundation; representatives from Osteotech and ARC Tissue Services; and various reproductive experts. Other contributing organizations included the FDA, CDC, Health Care Finance Administration (HFCA), Health Resources and Services Administration (HRSA), and National Heart, Lung, and Blood Institute (NHLBI). This was one of the most important documents in the history of donation and transplantation.

The Genesis of the Certified Tissue Banking Specialist Designation and Exam

During the late 1980s, "there wasn't a national certification program for tissue bank personnel," said Dr. Kagan, "so the AATB felt there needed to be a national exam to demonstrate a core knowledge base and proficiency." Consequently, in 1988, to improve quality by providing a measurement to show that personnel who worked in tissue banks were competent and adequately trained, the Association contracted to independently validate examinations developed to ascertain the knowledge of tissue bank employees. Job analysis surveys were commissioned periodically to determine the subject areas and their distribution within the exams in order to remain relevant and keep up with federal, state, and professional expectations and fluctuations.

Paula Applegate, originally a surgical nurse and a manager with the American Red Cross Tissue Services and now a semi-retired compliance control coordinator at MTF, was one of the first. "Twenty- seven years ago I started with the American Red Cross, and we did full-service tissue banking: I did donor development, medical histories and consent, recovery, cadaveric and living donors, and distribution to surgeons. The American Red Cross did their own processing at the time at different locations, so I was not familiar with that. Now people often only do one job, recovery or screening, but we were jacks of all trades."

"In those days the AATB had the standards and a technical manual and you had to answer questions. The exam wasn't a criterion for my job, but the American Red Cross was supportive of us studying for, getting, and maintaining our certification."

"One of the motivating factors for certification was to make sure the technicians had a certain level of education," said cryotechnologist Russ Bierbaum of ReproTech. "The AATB was devoted to education."

"It was very well done in terms of the reliability and validity of the exam," said Dr. Kagan. Individuals who passed were awarded the CTBS or CRCS certification, which immediately became a vital qualification for tissue bank professionals and remains so to this day.

Regulatory Matters

In the early 1990s, partially as a result of the maturity of the profession and partially in response to the emergence of certain infectious diseases, the AATB significantly increased the number of educational meetings, workshops, and symposia around the country. The content of the AATB's training and education added a second focus on quality and regulatory matters to its traditional one of screening donors and processing tissue.

In 1993, the sixth release of the *Standards* added a new section entitled "Medical Facility Tissue Storage and Issuance." This section was designed to help medical facilities by offering structural and functional guidelines for the handling of human tissue allografts and autografts. This edition also incorporated tissue-specific standards derived from the tissue-specific technical manuals originally developed in the late 1980s.

By the seventh version (1996), the AATB *Standards* had grown from 21 pages to a book of 108 pages. It included sections such as "Records Management," "Release and Transfer of Tissues," "General Operations" (i.e., procedure manual, staff training/competency, safety practices, and facilities/equipment requirements), and "Quality Assurance and Quality Control."

The *Standards* were not only getting bigger; they were also getting more difficult to produce. With the field expanding so rapidly, "one of the problems was in having a group of people to agree upon a standard," said orthopedic surgeon Dr. Michael Joyce. "Most of the time we agreed on the best practice," but the complexity and advancement of the field was making it more difficult.

A Major Achievement

In the mid-1990s, Jeanne Mowe and then–AATB president Dr. Ted Eastlund met with the Joint Commission on Accreditation, Health Care and Certification, an independent, not-for-profit organization that accredits and certifies nearly 21,000 healthcare organizations and programs in the United States. Mowe and Dr. Eastlund explained that the AATB standards could be used to properly track, handle, and store tissue and report adverse reactions. As a result, The Joint Commission eventually put those kinds of requirements in their accreditation program, but initially it was only inserted in the laboratory section, because, at that time, the laboratory was the department that often stored tissue. These standards were later expanded and now appear in five department accreditation compliance manuals used by The Joint Commission.

"Today, I view the development of The Joint Commission's tissue standards as one of the biggest successes to the promotion of tissue safety in the U.S.," said Scott Brubaker, senior vice president of policy, AATB. "The AATB president and the executive director raised awareness with a professional society that accredits healthcare facilities nationwide. It led to widespread improvement of the safe handling of tissue by end users. The impact over 20 years, although not formally measured, has likely been immense."

Accreditation

The accreditation program, which was begun in 1986 and bolstered with AATB certification of professions, and its education and training programs continued to be the highest of priorities for the AATB in the late 1980s and through the 1990s. There were still, however, "a number of tissue banks who were not following AATB standards," said David Campagnari. In response, the Association sought ways to incentivize tissue banks to seek accreditation. "More and more," said Joel Osborne, a quality control specialist first with the American Red Cross and then with MTF, "some hospitals wouldn't accept tissue if the bank wasn't accredited. But there wasn't a membership benefit to being accredited." The AATB Board therefore extended to employees of accredited institutions benefits of membership such as discounted registrations for meetings and educational offerings; discounted *Standards*; and the opportunity to participate in AATB councils, committees, and elections to voice opinions and needs and to collaborate with other members.

Overall, the continuing push for accreditation seemed to work. Between 1986 and 1989, 17 tissue banks earned accreditation. By 1999, the number had grown to 67. "The accreditation program has continued to benefit the tissue industry with recipient safety and pushing the emphasis on quality and safety," said Dr. Michael Joyce.

Independent Inspectors

The inspections of tissue banks that the AATB had initiated in the 1980s were always a critical part of the accreditation process, and, as previously mentioned, the AATB had originally handled them internally. "When I first started," said Bierbaum, "the inspectors were our colleagues and our peer inspectors."

"The very first accreditations relied on peer audits," echoed Osborne. "So, for example, when the MTF was first accredited in the early 90s, the auditors came from other tissue banks… which was a little bit strange, but it worked."

Consistency was the initial concern. "I was co-chair of the first AATB Inspection and Accreditation Committee," said Dr. Kagan. "We knew that if we were going out and performing inspections, they all had to be based on the same criteria, so we initiated a mandatory training course and checklist for all inspectors. If one set of inspectors went to one facility and another set went to another facility, both facilities had to demonstrate compliance with the same criteria."

Dr. Emmanuel Tayo, was a neuro-pharmacologist hired in 1996 by then–President Dr. Michael Joyce as AATB's first inspector. "A tissue bank would undergo a re-inspection once every three years," said Osborne. "It really was very helpful—especially to tissue banks that are relatively new, to prepare for other inspections like FDA inspections."

In 1998, Tayo passed away, and Dr. Joyce called on Dr. Robert Stevenson, then retired, to review the accreditation program. Dr. Stevenson assembled a manual for the accreditation process and hired retired FDA inspectors to take up the work. "It all began to roll," said Dr. Stevenson, "when people understood we conducted our reviews with impartiality and evenhandedness. The banks didn't want other tissue banks reviewing them, and they realized we would protect their proprietary information in our reports."

"The peer-to-peer review and inspection process was good, but switching to outside contractors to do the inspections was better," said Lou Barnes, president and COO with UMTB Biomedical in Florida and, in 2016, AATB's chair-elect. "Presenting blind findings to the accreditation committee for voting was a big step forward, removing the perception of any conflict of interest from the prior process." Many feel the professionalism inherent in independent assessment to be one of the most important contributions that the association has made to the healthcare industry.

FDA Building

The FDA Formally Enters the Process

Almost since its inception in 1976, the AATB had been anticipating that the FDA would eventually regulate tissue banking. Speculation about the FDA's intentions increased after 1986, when AATB founder Dr. Ken Sell, by then the scientific director of the National Institute of Allergy and Infectious Diseases, invited Dr. Henry "Hank" Meyer at the Bureau of Biologics of the FDA to an AATB meeting to discuss the prospect of regulation of tissue banks by the FDA.

Dr. Meyer accepted the invitation and subsequently expressed his opinion that, because tissue banking was in its infancy, regulation at that time could restrict its development as an area of medical practice. He suggested instead that the FDA monitor the development and application of voluntary standards before imposing any federal regulations. From that point forward, long before formal federal regulations were ever developed, the AATB and the FDA met periodically and informally regarding the development and application of voluntary standards for tissue banking.

A Beta Test: Allograft Heart Valves

About this time, as tissue transplantation grew more sophisticated, the line between tissues and medical devices began to blur.[21] It is a critical distinction, as devices are subject to expensive and lengthy clinical trials that tissues are not. "If you develop a new product," said Dr. Tomford, "like a new device that doctors use, or a new drug with which they are going to treat hypertension, that device or drug has to go through an extremely rigorous and expensive process to be approved by the FDA. That's not the case with tissue. As long as they are only minimally modified, tissue is not subject to this process and therefore can reach the public in a more efficient and accelerated manner."

As a natural part of the human body, in other words, tissue was assumed to

Allograft Heart Valve

be safe. However, donated tissue can be processed in a way that could make it categorized as a medical device.

In the mid-1980s, against this backdrop of increasingly sophisticated processing of tissue, a number of tissue banks started working in the field of allograft heart valve cryopreservation.

Unexpectedly, the FDA announced that cryopreserved allograft heart valves would be regulated as Class III medical devices, and an investigational device exemption (IDE) and subsequent premarket approval (PMA) would be required in order to continue distributing this type of human tissue. In response, a number of tissue banks chose to work together to create a multiple-sponsor clinical study program to meet the FDA's requirement for an IDE and eventual PMA. These tissue banks also worked together to challenge the FDA's regulatory scheme for allograft heart valves. "We really wanted the FDA to focus their efforts on safety of tissues for transplant," said David Campagnari, one of the AATB members involved, "rather than on the efficacy of cryopreserved human heart valves."

Ultimately, after more than two and a half years of the tissue banks challenging the FDA's process by utilizing legal processes and seeking assistance from the U.S. Congress, the FDA decided to change the regulatory requirements for cryopreserved human heart valves. "In short," said Campagnari, "the FDA canceled the requirement for an IDE/PMA and reclassified heart valves as Class II devices with special controls. We felt like that was a pretty major win."

The FDA Escalates Its Involvement

In 1991, the Centers for Disease Control and Prevention (CDC) reported transmission of HIV by human tissue. The tissue had been obtained from a donor who had tested as non-reactive to anti-HIV at the time of donation. Following reported HIV transmission in recipients of organs from this same

Dr. Ken Sell
Father of the AATB

If there is a father of the AATB, it is Dr. Kenneth Sell.

Born in Bismarck, North Dakota, in 1931, Sell was valedictorian of his graduating class in both his high school and at the University of North Dakota, where he was also voted the most outstanding alumnus. He earned his M.D. degree from Harvard University and his Ph.D. in immunopathology from the University of Cambridge, England.

From 1956 to 1977, he served in the U.S. Navy Medical Corps in Bethesda, beginning as the first director of the U.S. Navy Tissue Bank, which he personally lobbied Congress to found. He continued later as chairman of the Department of Experimental and Clinical Immunology and as commanding officer of the Naval Medical Research Institute.

In 1985, after his tour at NIH, he joined the Emory University faculty as pathology chair and as first director of Emory's Winship Cancer Center. Under Dr. Sell, Emory's pathology department grew to become one of the nation's largest programs for graduate training of pathologists and a major force for biomedical research.

Dr. Sell is one of the pioneers in the field of transplantation and tissue banking in particular, and the tissue bank symposium he organized in 1975 led to the formation of the AATB. In addition to being the founder, Dr. Sell was twice president of the Association. In recognition of his contributions, AATB endowed a yearly award in his name. He was also a founding member of the American Council on Transplantation.

"In his distinguished career, Dr. Ken Sell made significant contributions both as an immunologist and as a scientific administrator," said NIAID Director Dr. Anthony S. Fauci. "His work in the area of immunoregulation added to our understanding of several disciplines, including cancer, transplantation immunology, autoimmunity, and infectious diseases. NIAID benefitted greatly from his dedication and expertise."

Former NIAID Director Dr. Richard Krause noted that Dr. Sell oversaw "the implementation of biocontainment laboratory procedures for recombinant DNA research." NIAID alumnus Dr. Sheldon Cohen said that Dr. Sell was highly instrumental in the development of NIAID's serum bank for tissue typing. He also initiated the Introduction to Biomedical Research Program for gifted minority undergraduate students.

Dr. Sell was among the first to recognize the early threat of AIDS, and he started a program to gather blood and other bodily fluid samples from people with AIDS in order to store them for research. As scientific director of the National Institute of Allergy and Infectious Diseases in the early 80s, he quickly allocated researchers and resources to fight this disease. "We made the decision to look for every viral and bacterial infectious agent that we possibly could," he said. "We used every kind of technique and culture method we could trying to isolate the culprit."

During his career, he earned both the Legion of Merit Award and the Meritorious Service Medal during his Navy tour of duty. He received the Public Health Service Special Recognition Award for his service at NIH, and in 1992, the Naval Medical Research Institute honored him as the Most Distinguished Alumnus of the first 50 years.

In 1997, a symposium was organized to honor Dr. Sell's contributions to the field of tissue banking and to recount the many accomplishments that have occurred both during his participation in the field and thereafter. Many of the participants in the 1997 symposium had been contributors in the 1975 symposium.

Dr. Sell died in 1996.

(Partial source: https://nihrecord.nih.gov/PDF_Archive/1996%20PDFs/19961119.pdf, pg. 15)

donor, however, HIV-I was detected in the donor's stored lymphocytes, using viral culture and polymerase chain reaction (PCR) testing. Because of this transmission, the Association's focus turned more directly toward determining clinical and sociological risk factors in donor screening.[22]

Soon thereafter, the FDA received reports from U.S. tissue banks of brokers selling unprocessed tissue from improperly screened and tested donors from Russia, Eastern Europe, and Central and South America. "It was discovered that brokers were importing bodies and attempting to sell them as tissue donors that were accompanied by erroneous serology results," said Dr. Michael Joyce, "meaning the blood that was sent with a donor body wasn't really the donor's blood. The serology tests provided were wrong. They were either not matched to the donors, or sometimes they were falsified. The bodies being brokered were imported from South America[23] and Eastern Europe, to name a few sources."[24]

"At that point the FDA stepped in," said Dr. Ross Wilkins, Senior Medical Director of AlloSource in Denver.

A Symbiotic Relationship

Once engaged, the FDA soon realized that while it was their role to retain regulatory authority over tissue banking, the staff lacked the specific expertise in the field.

"They knew they needed to learn the science [of tissue banking]," said Dr. Wilkins. Recognizing that the AATB's understanding of the field far exceeded its own, and that it represented tissue banks across the country, the FDA thus made the fairly unprecedented proposal that it would work in concert with the AATB.

Starting in the mid-1990s, agreed Dr. Kagan, "the FDA relied heavily on us… and we relied on them, based on their experience in blood banking and rule-making, to help them as they helped us. It was very much a joint effort."

On December 10, 1993, the AATB published the following news release:

> David A. Kessler, M.D., Commissioner of the U.S. Food and Drug Administration, announced today that FDA intends to publish interim federal regulations regarding the procurement, processing, storage, and distribution of human tissue in the Federal Register early next week. According to Dr. Kessler, "The FDA is issuing regulations to strengthen Federal oversight over tissue transplantation, especially in the area of musculoskeletal tissue."
>
> FDA recently investigated the sale of imported musculoskeletal tissue materials intended for transplantation without adequate donor screening and testing procedures. The investigation revealed that tissue was acquired in cases where there was unsatisfactory medical history and lack of information about risk factors.
>
> In addition to the interim regulations, FDA will shortly propose additional mandatory regulations that require registration of all tissue banking establishments. The regulations will call for record keeping, informed consent, accurate labeling to permit tracking, and standard operating procedures.
>
> Finally, FDA has issued an Import Alert. No one should import any tissues into the United States without first contacting the FDA's Office of Health Affairs. "No one," warns Dr. Kessler, "should use tissues from any source, in the absence of an adequate medical history of the donor and appropriate screening and testing."

AATB Supports FDA's Effort

FDA's announcement of interim final regulations governing the operation of tissue banks is an appropriate, measured response to real—but, we believe, isolated—problems with a small number of suppliers of tissues. We support the agency's actions, which are intended to assure that all tissues provided for surgical use in *the United States are both safe and structurally sound. These goals have been at the center of AATB's activities from the beginning; indeed, they are the reason for AATB's formation.*

The FDA started with musculoskeletal tissue, though Russ Bierbaum noted the general feeling that they would soon include other kinds of tissue. The point was that tissue banking was no longer on its own, but the general consensus was that the safety for tissue recipients would be improved with FDA involvement. It was also clear that AATB could have an impact on the creation of FDA regulations and subsequent enforcement if AATB continued to be engaged with the FDA.

After publishing its Interim Final Rule on human tissue intended for transplantation[25] in 1993, the FDA's Center for Biologics Evaluation and Research (CBER), which regulates biological products for human use, was assigned responsibility for oversight of tissue establishments that screen donors and recover, process, store, and/or distribute tissue for transplantation. This Interim Rule included minimum requirements for screening and testing tissue donors and for maintaining procedures and records with specific emphasis on preventing the transmission of viral hepatitis and HIV.

Despite the earlier heart valve lawsuit, the AATB and the Eye Bank Association of America (EBAA) actively promoted the continuation of this communication between industry professionals and CBER to ensure further development of regulations would be effective, and the relationship became increasingly symbiotic. AATB accreditation individuals were invited to address an FDA inspectors workshop in 1995, and eventually further meetings were set up between the two organizations. "I remember us going to the FDA and actually giving a day's presentation covering the AATB's standards," said Dr. Joyce. Various public workshops and meetings were held.

From this point forward, neither organization would issue any important pronouncements without considering the other. After the Interim Rule of 1993, the AATB *Standards* included content from the FDA's HCT/P regulations, specifically emphasizing the tissue bank's responsibility regarding donor screening and testing and the provision of all aspects related to maintaining an effective quality program.

In 1997, the FDA published an "Approach to Regulation of Cellular & Tissue-Based Products," and then a "Final Rule and Guidance Document for Human Tissue Intended for Transplantation" that amended parts of the Interim Rule. The "Final Rule" focused on considerations involving the eligibility of deceased donors and required "human cell, tissue, and cellular and tissue-based product (HCT/P) establishments to screen and test cell and tissue donors for risk factors for, and clinical evidence of, relevant communicable disease agents and diseases."[26]

When the FDA published the "Proposed Approach to the Regulation of Cellular and Tissue-based Products" in February 1997, it served as the blueprint needed to implement the approach, including prescribed time frames for planned actions. In 1998, the FDA Center for Biologics Evaluation and Research published a Tissue Action Plan, which was the manifestation of this blueprint, and which recognized that innovation in the field would only increase and propose "a new approach to the regulation of human cellular and tissue-based products." The Tissue Action Plan recognized that advancements in biotechnology would continue to "enhance and expand the use of human cells and tissues as therapeutic products." It offered a new regulatory framework providing:

> *a unified approach to the regulation of both traditional and new products. Regulation would focus on three general areas: 1) preventing unwitting use of contaminated tissues with the*

potential for transmitting infectious diseases such as AIDS and hepatitis; 2) preventing improper handling or processing that might contaminate or damage tissues; 3) ensuring that clinical safety and effectiveness is demonstrated for tissues that are highly processed, are used for other than their normal function, are combined with non-tissue components, or are used for metabolic purposes.[27]

In describing the steps FDA would take to create a tissue framework and respond to various recommendations by other organizations, TAP has been instrumental in implementing the FDA's proposed framework for the regulation of human tissue.

The partnership between the FDA and the AATB worked, noted Dr. Wilkins, in large part because of Jeanne Mowe. "Jeanne served as the liaison to the FDA and other organizations. The good working relationship would not have happened without her. She was a peacemaker and had the ability to get people to talk and cooperate. Slowly a cooperative atmosphere and relationship developed, and the AATB ultimately did a wonderful job in working with the FDA."

In the end, "FDA involvement was mutually beneficial," said Dr. Joyce, "because if you pass AATB accreditation, then you should most likely pass the FDA inspection, and vice-versa. There is always a give and take, and one of us catches things the other doesn't, but I think tissue is certainly safer with the FDA involved."

A New Type of Processor

Perhaps the biggest change in the history of tissue banking since the founding of the AATB in 1976 has involved the introduction of for-profit tissue processors.

"The tissue banking field was originally a collection of non-profits and academic institutions spun from the Navy Tissue Bank," said Joel Osborne of MTF. Recovery of tissue has of course always been, and remains, a non-profit practice, but in the 1980s, as development of this tissue expanded into more and more sophisticated products that included allograft tissues, a few for-profit processors appeared. "There was one for-profit cardiovascular bank, but there weren't very many people competing in the cardiovascular area, so it really didn't matter," said Osborne. "And there was one for-profit skin processor which was not highly visible."

As time went on and technology advanced, and need for tissue increased, processors needed to invest in more and more infrastructure – labs, personnel, etc. – and to incur a great many costs to turn this donated tissue into more and more sophisticated products. As a consequence, commercial processors increased, although initially they were not readily accepted by the tissue community.

When the American Red Cross said it was going to take a leadership role in tissue banking in 1988 and use Osteotech, a private company, for processing, the tissue bank pioneers from the 1970s were somewhat alarmed at the apparent possibility that the profession might be tipping over to the for-profit side. "The people running Osteotech had come from the medical device side in New Jersey," said MTF CEO Bruce Stroever, "so they had an entirely different mind-set, approach, and, many thought, set of priorities than non-profit tissue bankers."

Needless to say, the prospect created concern. "This caused a big, big battle about whether or not it was appropriate for for-profits to be involved in processing donated human tissue," said Osborne.

"There was always some friction, because we didn't think shareholders should make money off an altruistic donation of tissue," agreed Dr. Joyce. "Obviously that has gone by the wayside. But I remember having discussions about this. Former AATB

President Dr. Ted Eastlund said commercial banks with stockholders were actually being given a dividend for their efforts. He was the most vocal individual against it."

The commercial processors changed the landscape of the tissue-banking world to some extent by generating competition among tissue banks. "Obviously tissue banks compete for donated tissues, and they compete for hospital customers that use the tissues," said Osborne, "so even though it is a non-profit field, it has its element of competition, just like hospitals may compete for patients. But the big non-profit tissue banks at the time, LifeNet, AlloSource, the Michigan Tissue Bank, clearly saw Osteotech as competition."

It took five or six years, but Osteotech's solid performance and quality earned them respect in the field. For instance, Osteotech developed Grafton, which is a demineralized bone tissue that can be processed into a number of different products, and take form as a putty or gel that is successfully used for different bone-related surgeries. "Grafton was good," said Dr. Michael Joyce. "That sort of changed some people's attitudes."

"It all stopped being an issue in the mid 90s," said Stroever. "Osteotech was a great processor. Eventually the fact that they were doing a good job, they were not causing disruption in the recovery field and not involved at all in the interface with families and donations… I think the resistance just petered out."

Shedding their stigma, for-profit entities began to proliferate. The University of Florida Tissue Bank became RTI, going from a non-profit to a for-profit in 1998. Others, like LifeCell and CryoLife also prospered. By 2000, the landscape had indeed changed: of the 58 federally designated organ procurement organizations in the U.S.,[28] many had a tie to a for-profit that created biological solutions such as bone, skin, and heart valves.

The Benefits of Working Together

The large tissue processors like CryoLife and Osteotech joined the traditional non-profit tissue banks in creating new tissue forms. There was a downside to the advances, however, for new technologies led to patents, which created, some thought, barriers to the traditional information sharing that had been a hallmark of the early years of the AATB.

Innovation also led to specialization, as different companies focused on processing specific types of tissue into products such as decellularized skin structures or bone products to enhance the allografts' ability to fuse with native bone. With the increasing competition, hospitals sought the most economical solutions, which drove more innovation and competition.

Nowadays, said Stroever, "some of the biggest tissue banks in the country are for-profit, like RTI. A lot of modest to midsize to large tissue banks are for-profit and there are a number of very large not-for-profits. The battles are long gone. We don't throw rocks at each other over who's for-profit and who's not."

"We've gone full circle," agreed Dr. Joyce, referring to this one element of tissue banking's departure from a purely non-profit ethos to return to the more traditional business of medicine, but he keeps the overall non-profit spirit of the profession top of mind. "When I give my talks to tissue banking physicians, I emphasize that we wouldn't have anything to work with if it wasn't for the altruistic donation of a particular donor or a donor designating what they wanted done once they die. Those are gifts, and we are expected to treat them as a gift."

The AATB Becomes More Widely Collaborative

With Jeanne Mowe extending the network in the 1990s, and with the

Jeanne Mowe
The AATB's First Executive Director

In 1983, AATB President Dr. Ken Sell recognized that the organization needed a full-time executive director, and found Jeanne Mowe, then the manager of the Public Information Office of the National Cancer Institute's Frederick (Maryland) Operations Division.

Dr. Sell—and the AATB—lucked out, for "Jeanne Mowe was a dynamo," in the words of Glenn Greenleaf. In addition to effectively managing daily office operations, Mowe threw her heart and soul into the Association's mission, serving as a 24/7 evangelist for tissue banking and transplantation, manning booths at conferences, distributing information, recruiting members, and connecting people across disciplines.

Former AATB President Dr. Rich Kagan said, "Jeanne Mowe was very important in my getting involved in AATB. She was an amazing person. If you were to ask my who was the most important person in my life with AATB I would say Jeanne Mowe. She sucked me in; she nurtured me; she gave everything."

The sentiment was echoed by many. "She took me under her wing," said incoming AATB President Lou Barnes, "and from then on I've been an active engaged member of the association. It all started with Jeanne."

"She knew all the right people," said Dr. Kagan. "She was respected by everyone. Jeanne was the heart of the organization. She had connections with NIH, the Blood Bank, the blood industry. All those things were huge in the growth and development of the organization."

One of Mowe's greatest contributions, said AATB Policy Chief Scott Brubaker, involved her participation in taking AATB *Standards* to The Joint Commission and getting them to incorporate them in their manuals for hospitals.

In 1999, Mowe supported the hiring of Bob Rigney. "She wanted the AATB to hire somebody who eventually became her boss," said Russ Bierbaum. "It's not often that someone suggests hiring someone to take over what you are doing and be your boss. But she knew that for the betterment of the AATB, we needed to move to the next level."

Mowe was appointed to the Surgeon General's Task Force on Organ Donation (1991–92) and the executive committee of the American Council on Transplantation (1989–91), the Technical/Scientific Workshop Committee of the American Association of Blood Banks, the American Society for Testing and Materials (ASTM), and the College of Biology Editors. Unfortunately, she took ill and passed away in 2003. Jeanne de Chantal Mowe left a legacy, through fostering the AATB in its early years, of helping countless tissue recipients who will never her know her name, her selfless attitude, or her many contributions to tissue banking.

FDA and AATB starting to work closely together, the AATB began to work closely with many other organizations. After the turn of the century, the Association partnered with the AABB (formerly known as the American Association of Blood Banks) and the Eye Bank Association of America (EBAA) to develop a reference handbook. "We worked with the AABB on development of a tissue management handbook for end users of tissue to promote best practice for 'safe handling of tissue' in hospitals, whether it was managed by the blood transfusion service or by the surgical (operating room) staff," said Scott Brubaker.

During the 1990s, the Association collaborated with the American Burn Association, the American Orthopaedic Society for Sports Medicine (AOSSM), and the American Academy of Orthopaedic Surgeons (AAOS), with the latter endorsing the use of allograft tissue that was sourced only from tissue banks that were accredited by the AATB.

Legal Milestones

As the millennium neared, it became obvious the need for tissue banking was growing rapidly. For instance, bone allograft distribution alone had doubled from 200,000 in 1994 to 400,000 in 1997, and would reach 600,000 by the year 2000.[29] Consequently, the federal government sought to increase donation rates with the National Organ and Tissue Donation Initiative in December of 1997. This initiative required all Medicare-participating hospitals to refer all deaths and imminent deaths to an organ procurement organization (OPO), a tissue bank, or an eye bank. According to the Department of Health and Human Services, this practice alone resulted in a 5.6 percent increase in donation.[30]

Analyzing the Mission and a New President and CEO

In the mid-1990s, while the AATB was building its relationship with the FDA, and during Dr. Randy May's term as president, AATB's membership consisted largely of individual tissue bankers. This reflected the landscape in the 1970s and much of the 1980s. The larger tissue banks, however, like LifeNet, MTF, and AlloSource, which had emerged over the past decade, began to feel that their institutional needs, and monitoring the industry as a whole, warranted as high a priority for the AATB as did meeting the needs of the individual members and the traditional activities of educating, training, and certifying technicians. Consequently, May organized the strategic planning meeting that ran over the course of a year, and which led to a proposal that the bylaws be changed so that the tissue banks would get extra votes on all issues. Not surprisingly, this led to a concern that the big banks were trying to take over tissue banking. The discourse was animated.

"A lot of energy went into exploring changes to the governance," said Dr. Michael Joyce, Dr. May's successor and the president from 1997 to 1999. "We had meetings with outside consultants, but when the dust settled any significant change in governance was voted down 75 percent to 25 percent." The issue would arise again in future years, but in the meantime, Dr. Joyce focused on unity, bringing Association members together to speak with one voice on a variety of regulatory, safety, and donor suitability issues.

By 1999, the organization had grown enough that it needed more administrative help. "Jeanne Mowe was the executive director, and well connected with the FDA and with people in Washington," said Dr. Joyce, but even she felt additional skills would help the organization. Mowe recommended that the AATB hire someone with strong business skills to help usher in this era of growth.

In June of that year, the AATB hired P. Robert Rigney, an attorney with past experience at the American Association of Blood Banks and as director of the Washington, D.C.-based regulatory affairs office of the American Academy of Dermatology. Mowe remained on and worked alongside Rigney for the next five years until an illness led to her passing in 2003.

At the millennium, the AATB had clearly fulfilled Dr. Ken Sell's original vision, with more than 1,200 individual members and more than 60 accredited tissue banks. "One thing I will always remember about the AATB," said Bierbaum: "even though tissue banks were competitors, we were cooperative, shared information for the betterment of the industry and tissue recipients. I think that is pretty unusual in professional organizations… We shared our successes or failures or problems with each other so that we could all be more successful and be able to provide a better service to the community. That was the strength of the AATB."

Amniotic Tissue Donation from One Mother Helps Another Mother Heal

Fifteen years of dancing left Ashleigh with a painful bone spur and degenerative arthritis in her first metatarsophalangeal joint, which made it difficult to keep up with her young son, Beckett.

"As a dancer, you're really hard on your feet," said Ashleigh. "Sometimes you power through an injury when you should be taking care of it, so I'm sure at some point I injured my foot and then it just got progressively worse."

As her foot condition made it more and more difficult to stay active and chase Beckett around, she knew she needed to see a doctor, who then suggested surgery to help correct the problem.

During the procedure, her surgeon removed the bone spur and then used a product derived from human amniotic membrane from a donated placenta directly following an elective C-section to cover the cartilage degradation on her joint. Amniotic membrane is rich in growth factors and can be used as a protective barrier following surgical intervention.

Though she won't return to dancing, Ashleigh's surgery helped alleviate her pain so she can be more active. Indeed, Ashleigh is back on her feet and keeping up with Beckett. She looks forward to running, biking, and enjoying time outside with her family.

Ashleigh Deal with her husband Chad and their son, Beckett

When Ashleigh reflected on the donor of the tissue she received, she said, "It was inspiring to know that someone made a decision to help me without knowing me, which speaks to the selflessness and generosity of all donors."

CHAPTER THREE: CHALLENGES, COLLABORATION, AND CONTRACTORS: TAKING THE NEXT STEP, 1987–2000

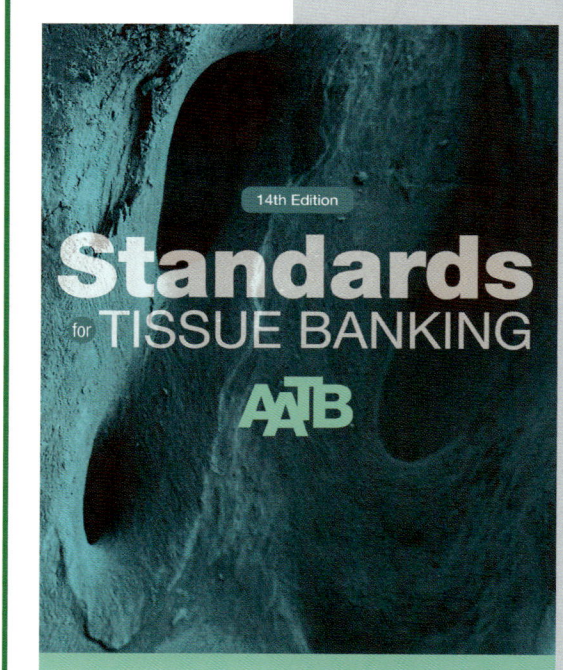

The AATB *Standards*

Chapter Four:
Technology, Growth, Consolidation, and Globalization, 2000–Present

Responding to the FDA

Despite a good working relationship with the FDA, over-regulation remained a concern and an ongoing priority for the AATB at the turn of the millennium. "We formed special committees and work groups to represent our profession's track record of safety and standard setting to those in Congress and the FDA in order to protect our regulatory classification," said Lou Barnes of UMTB Biomedical. "Our safety record was good, and continues to be so good. Our concern with the FDA was regulatory overreach; risk-based analysis failed to justify the increased amount of regulation that they wanted for the work that we do."

A side benefit of forming new work groups, he noted, was in getting "more new folks volunteering to serve on these work committees and expanding the talent pool in the association."

Bruce Stroever, head of MTF, echoed the overall sentiment. "Given the volume, three or four problems in a decade is a phenomenally low number. We had this argument with the FDA all the time. They kept talking about tighter rules, and we kept saying, 'What are you concerned about? What is the problem that you are trying to solve? Because tissue is the safest implant that you can possibly get.' We made that point to the FDA over and over again."

AATB Senior Vice President of Policy Scott Brubaker emphasized the AATB's proactive approach to this same issue. "One way we work with regulators is by developing useful, well-thought comments and submitting them to FDA before rules and guidance concerning

HCT/Ps are finalized" he said.

Updating and Extending the Standards

The Association not only continued to update and improve the *Standards*, but also sought for the first time to include others in the process, rather than after the fact. "We made significant changes in the AATB *Standards* and in the membership of the *Standards* Committee while I led the committee," said Francis Hornicek, MD, PhD, of Massachusetts General Hospital, the chair of the *Standards* Committee in the early 2000s, and president of the AATB from 2007 to 2009. "One of the biggest of these changes involved having representatives of the FDA and the CDC join AATB's *Standards* Committee. We didn't have them on the committee originally, and so we would make decisions and have to talk to them afterwards. So I said, 'Why not just include them and have them part of our committees?'"

The establishment of the Scientific and Technical Affairs Committee (STAC) was another innovation, designed to "promote, explore and advance scientific questions" and "postulate innovative solutions" and to be the "primary source of scientific and technical guidance"[31] for the AATB. That guidance would ultimately be translated into improvement in the standards, which aspired to cover more than what the federal regulations (FDA) covered or required. "We were the trendsetters for the establishment of more scientific committees to improve the standards," said Dr. Hornicek.

An article in the June 2004 New England Journal of Medicine, "Infections Transmitted through Musculoskeletal-Tissue Allografts," written by two physicians from the Mayo Clinic College of Medicine in Rochester, Minnesota, agreed that the AATB *Standards* "go beyond the requirements of the FDA." This article also concluded with recommendations, the most notable of which was that, "All tissue banks should be accredited by the AATB."

The AATB also had help from others. "By 2005 there was more and more tissue being transplanted, and it was mostly stored for later use in the operating room of a hospital, by surgical centers and by blood transfusion services," said Scott Brubaker. "The Joint Commission decided to expand the tissue standards it had adopted in the 1990s to be included in five different accreditation manuals. In many of the healthcare facilities in the US, these safe tissue handling standards became commonplace." Dental offices also order, store and use certain, small-sized tissue allografts such as demineralized bone matrix, and the AATB has begun work with the American Dental Association (ADA) to educate their membership regarding safe tissue handling/tracking methods.

New Challenges: Diseases and Administrative Responses

The AATB has had occasional problems with inaccuracies propagated by the media. In 2000, an article in the Orange County Register about skin banking led to a *60 Minutes* piece, entitled "Skin and Bones," about an alleged national skin shortage. "I was the medical director of a skin bank with 500 square feet of skin available for transplantation and nobody called us," said Dr. Kagan. "But the journalists deduced that because it was a local problem in Orange County, it must be a national problem."

Dr. Kagan was president of the AATB at the time, and a member of the American Burn Association, which represents burn centers and burn surgeons. He was later appointed chair of a skin substitute taskforce, which was charged with ensuring the availability of human donor skin for transplantation in burn patients. "The people at *60 Minutes* were well on their way to their story, and the AATB couldn't collect the data fast enough to refute claims that there was insufficient donor skin for burn victims. The *60 Minutes* investigators should have asked more about whether the doctors in California tried to call any of the more than 50 skin banks listed in the ABA's Burn Care Resources Directory, which listed contact information for all U.S. and Canadian burn centers and tissue banks. Nobody asked those important questions. It was not good thorough and balanced investigative journalism."

Certain events such as transmission of disease via transplantation, also provided challenges that eventually altered professional standards. In a June 2004 article in *The New England Journal of Medicine*, "Clostridium Infections Associated with Musculoskeletal-Tissue Allografts," Dr. Marion Kainer, an investigator formerly with the Centers for Disease Control and Prevention, reported that the investigation at a tissue bank was prompted by the death of a 23-year-old man from Clostridium sordellii sepsis following knee surgery and transplantation of a musculoskeletal allograft. The article focused on 14 patients, all of whom had allegedly received Clostridium-contaminated allografts processed by a particular tissue bank. The article made several recommendations to reduce the risk of infection. These tragic incidents highlight a challenge that underscores the need to follow the highest professional standards follow AATB *Standards* and work with tissue banks accredited by the AATB. "The Clostridium infection was a sentinel event," said Dr. Hornicek.

Cases like this were also the impetus for requiring the use of the HCV NAT assay for all tissue donors and for sharing donor eligibility information. As a result, the AATB required donor testing using HIV-1 NAT and HCV NAT during 2003, two and a half years before FDA mandated them in May 2005.

In recent years, new viruses like West Nile, Ebola, and Zika have required extraordinary speed when it comes to making changes that keep patients safe from infection from tissue transplants. In many cases, the AATB and other organizations have proven more nimble than the FDA.

"When the Ebola virus became a concern in the US, we quickly developed a donor screening questionnaire template for review by our Physicians' Council and other stakeholders," said Brubaker. "With the assistance of representatives from the organ, tissue and eye banking associations, as well as federal authorities, we hashed through [protocols related to Ebola] in two weeks to get to a final version, and then issued it. So that was pretty quick. Within thirty days we created an addendum to the Uniform Donor Risk Assessment Interview form (UDRAI), with instructions and flow charts for screening a potential donor who may have returned to the U.S. after assisting with the Ebola outbreak in West Africa," stated Brubaker, who noted the existence of a stakeholder review group of about 30 people, including representatives from the CDC, Health Canada, FDA, and HRSA, which reviews and approves all such new protocols. "It's difficult for the FDA to move very fast," he said, "but they saw what we were doing for evaluating Ebola risk and appeared to let us take the lead for that occurrence of disease risk."

West Nile virus required a different approach, said Brubaker. "We've been working with the CDC to determine if West Nile Virus testing (WNV NAT) is relevant for a donor of tissue from a cadaver, or even from a living donor, because there has not been a transmission from tissue recorded during endemic periods or any period. The FDA has held off on requiring WNV NAT, but they could tell us to do that in another final guidance if they have a reason to do so. They continue to address relevant emerging infectious diseases."

There have continued to be, as always, some non-medical, or sociological challenges. One question involves the age-old problem of reporting. Do physicians or surgeons regularly report all adverse outcomes related to transplantation? It is simply a question of record-keeping and communication, but without proper reporting it is impossible to get accurate statistics or to spot emerging trends.

"There has been a lot of discussion about traceability and tracking tissues," said Brubaker. "Our tissue banks put a unique number on grafts, but what does the hospital, or the dentist office, or the surgical center do with that? Can they track the tissue if, for instance, there is a recall for whatever reason? Our members bring the expertise and experience needed, and improving the ability of end users to track tissue is a specific goal."

To help address this, in 2010 the World Health Organization created Project Notify, in which the AATB is involved as a consultant. The project created the Notify Library to raise awareness for cell and tissue banking professionals, physicians and allograft recipients to look for transmission of disease and report it. "The Notify Library contains reports of instances where there has been an adverse reaction or adverse event worldwide involving the use of blood, organs, tissues and cells," said Brubaker.

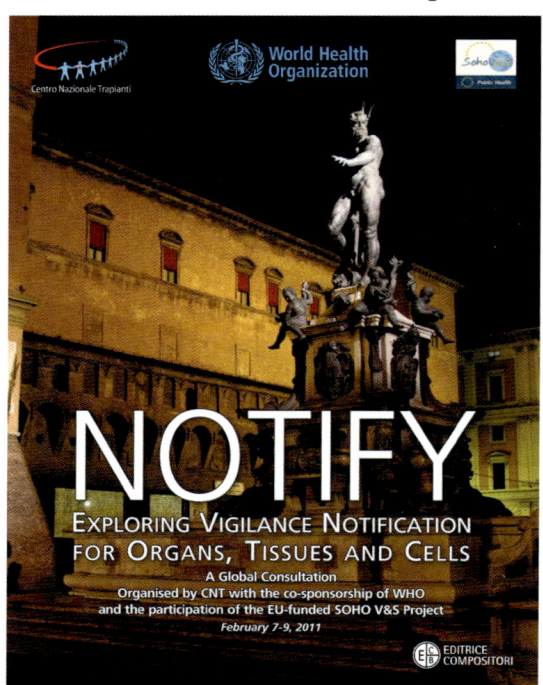

"The end users, the clinicians, may not know how to properly recognize a potential transmission of disease, so there is another guidance document that AATB is developing to fill that gap. Both the CDC and FDA bring knowledge and experience to these projects. We share a good relationship with them, and we are working together on different things. They're great partners."

Today, everyone, including the AATB, is vulnerable to the vagaries of the internet, so the need to have sophisticated public relations policies and capabilities represents a priority going forward.

Consolidation

With transplantation continuing to grow rapidly, the number of AATB-accredited tissue banks has continued to climb from 64 in 1998 to 133 in 2016. That is actually deceptively slow, for this growth has occurred in spite of many banks consolidating, leading to smaller banks disappearing into larger ones. In recent years MTF acquired the American Red Cross, and LifeNet recently acquired Northwest Tissue Bank. AlloSource acquired several banks, and CTS in Dayton, Ohio, has acquired eight. Indeed, in the last 25 years these four banks, along with Acelity (formerly LifeCell), CryoLife, LifeLink Tissue Bank, MiMedx, RTI Surgical, and University of Miami Tissue Bank (UMTB) have grown into the largest tissue processors today, as soon below. All of them except MiMedx had their start before the new millennium.

Acelity (Formerly LifeCell)

LifeCell, now headquartered in Branchburg, New Jersey, has united with Kinetics Concepts Incorporated and Systagenix to become Acelity, a global wound care company with 5,800 employees in 80 countries. To date, LifeCell has provided over one million dermal grafts for procedures ranging from complex hernia repair to breast reconstruction following mastectomy.

AlloSource

Now one of the world's largest processor of cellular bone allografts, Allosource has nearly 500 employees and an international footprint.

CryoLife, Inc.

In the last five years, CryoLife has acquired Cardiogenesis Corporation, a pioneer in the development and use of laser technology for transmyocardial revascularization (TMR) in patients with severe angina, and On-X Life Technologies Holdings, Inc., the leading manufacturer of artificial heart valve replacement and repair products. Now a multi-national company that occupies a 200,000 sq. ft. corporate headquarters on a 21-acre campus in northwest Atlanta, CryoLife has over 500 employees and sales representatives in over 75 countries.

Community Tissue Services (CTS)

CTS in Dayton, Ohio has over 500 employees, and operates regional offices in California, Texas, Indiana, Tennessee, Pennsylvania, Oregon and Ohio, and two satellite offices in Idaho and Oregon. The organization annually distributes over 160,000 tissue grafts to over 2,000 hospitals, physicians and surgeons.

LifeLink Tissue Bank

Florida's LifeLink Tissue Bank operating for the last ten years out of new offices at Delaney Creek is today the largest not-for-profit tissue bank in the Southeast and one of the largest in the United States. It is part of a larger foundation that includes 3 OPO's, an immunology lab, and the tissue bank. LifeLink employs approximately 150 personnel and currently place approx. 50,000 allografts/year and recover roughly 1100 donors from OPO's, which include LifeLink of Georgia, LifeLink of Florida, and LifeLink of Puerto Rico. LifeLink also has a recovery contract with Translife that covers the Orlando service area. In its history it has placed over a million allografts with no transmission of disease or infection.

LifeNet Health

In 2007, on its 25th anniversary, LifeNet, changed its name to LifeNet Health. As of 2016, it has nearly 900 employees and distributes over a half a million individual implants every year and still serves as the OPO for most of Virginia.

MiMedx

The MiMedx Group, Inc. was incorporated on February 28, 2008. In 2011, it acquired Surgical Biologics, LLC, which used modern proprietary processing techniques to placental tissue to create unique ophthalmic, spinal, orthopedic, and dental implants. This strategic acquisition brought together amnion tissue processing technology with MiMedx's management team and extensive distribution network. After the acquisition, MiMedx consolidated the corporate offices and operating facilities in Kennesaw, Georgia.

Musculoskeletal Foundation (MTF)

In recent years MTF's mission has expanded to include the development of increasingly technologically advanced tissues, which are processed from musculoskeletal tissues, adult stem cells and skin. It also has affiliations with many medical device companies. To date, MTF states that it has recovered tissue from over 115,000 donors and provided over seven million allografts to surgeons, hospitals, dentists, clinicians and their patients since 1987.

RTI

RTI has processed over five million biologic implants for use in sports medicine, general surgery, and spine, orthopedic, trauma and cardiothoracic procedures in nearly 50 countries. It proudly cites zero confirmed incidence of implant-associated infection.

UMTB Biomedical, Inc.

In 2011, UMTB relocated to a new space of 55,000 sq. feet and 11 OR suites on the first and second floor of the University of Miami Life Science and Technology Park. Vivex Biomedical Inc. acquired UMTB in 2014. Today UMTB focuses on core products and new technologies to meet the ever growing biologic needs of surgeons and patients while continuing our 45-year history of serving and honoring donor and tissue recipients. UMTB has distributed more than 2,000,000 million allografts to over 18 countries, provided training for personnel from other tissue banks in the U.S. and foreign countries, and assisted in the organization of new tissue banks in the United States and abroad.

Unique Operating Models

Although these organizations all fall into either the for-profit or non-profit categories, operating models vary. UMTB is the only one still under the umbrella of a single university, and some, such as MTF, LifeNet and CTS also serve as local OPOs. AlloSource is especially unique, as it is owned by a consortium of six OPOs, managed by six Corporate Members: Donor Alliance in Denver, Colorado; Gift of Hope Organ & Tissue Donor Network in Chicago, Illinois; Iowa Donor Network in North Liberty, Iowa; LifeGift in Houston, Texas; Mid-America Transplant in St. Louis, Missouri; and Unyts in Buffalo, NY. These organizations

aopo
association of organ procurement organizations

The Association of Organ Procurement Organizations (AOPO) is a nonprofit organization recognized as the national representative of the fifty-eight federally-designated Organ Procurement Organizations committed to enhancing the quality, effectiveness and integrity of the donation process.

provide donated tissue from all over the country. "It's a case of the recovery side merging with the processing and distribution side," said Sue Dunn, CEO of one of the six OPOs that own AlloSource. "It works well."

Part of the consolidation in recent years is a result of increased competition between tissue banks for donors and for markets for their products. Fortunately, however, as Tom Cycyota said, "At the end of the day, the major tissue banks all have outstanding processing techniques. Safety and quality is no different." And as Cycyota pointed out the power of the mission often overrides the competition. "We have a joint venture with CTS. We work closely with LifeLink Tissue Bank in Florida. One time another tissue bank was caught in a weather situation, and FedEx couldn't get in or out because the airport was closed. We took their donor tissues for a while. It would have been tragic to lose those gifts. We're all committed to the mission above anything else."

Responding to a Changing Landscape

There has been another, perhaps inevitable trend. Increasing transplantation in other countries has driven the practice of distribution from local to national to international in scope. In the 2000s, the AATB sought to keep up. "I tried to make sure that we were looked at as a leading organization for representation of tissue banking internationally," said Dr. Hornicek. "It's not something that happens overnight but it is occurring. It is one of the main objectives."

Growth overseas actually began in the 1980s and 1990s. "The European Association of Tissue Banks, or EATB, grew out of the AATB," said Dr. William Tomford. Our colleagues in Asia have started an Asian Pacific Association of Tissue Banks which is thriving. We have international guests at the AATB meeting, and we attend meetings in Europe and Asia." Today, the AATB also has accredited tissue banks in Canada,

Singapore and South Korea.

On a global scale, the World Health Organization has provided guidance in a variety of areas, and the World Union of Tissue Banking Associations, has provided a forum for connecting with tissue banking associations and tissue banks around the world. The AATB, however, remains a leader.

"The AATB has reached a level of global recognition," said David Campagnari. "I think Scott Brubaker deserves a lot of credit for that. He was the one who really reached out to many other regulatory and standards setting groups to help them realize the value of what AATB was doing with standards and accreditation. I think that was really a turning point for the organization: the commitment the organization made in creating such a position and appointing Scott to this important leadership role."

Adding Priorities

The AATB has always served as a resource to help members adapt to changes in the profession. In the 1990s, the AATB added a focus on quality and regulatory matters to the initial priorities of education, training, accreditation, certification and safety. In 2007, when Dr. Francis Hornicek was president, the sheer size of the profession, as well as evolving technologies, dictated a new administrative structure. "When I became president of the AATB," said Dr. Hornicek, "we did a lot of strategic planning, and there were discussions about the future and how tissue banking should develop. We ended up making a shift from a member organization to more of a trade organization model." It still maintained the 501(c)3 non-profit status, of course, but this shift gave the major tissue banks a greater voice, and charged the AATB with monitoring legislation and working with the government, similar to a trade association.

Formation of the Tissue Policy Group

Building on this shift to a trade organization model, the major tissue banks sought to consolidate their influence in order to get representation for tissue banking as a whole in the health policy arena. "A few years ago, five or six of us who run the largest tissue banks in the country got together," said Bruce Stroever. "We agreed that we wanted to work inside the AATB, so we formed the Tissue Policy Group, which is now an AATB-chartered LLC. We decided to kick in our own money and hire a lobbyist and actually see if we couldn't improve our reputation in Washington and improve our position with the FDA and get the support that we needed for tissue banking."

The Tissue Policy Group was formed about 15 years after the earlier attempt in the late 1990s during May's tenure to achieve the same result. "The need to differentiate between individual tissue bankers and tissue banks was always there, but it took until 2012 or 2013 before we finally got that set up," said Stroever.

Today there is no competition between the tissue banks and the individual members. Both are important parts of the AATB, but "at least it gives the larger tissue banks that distribute probably 80 to 90 percent of the tissue in the country the ability to pool their resources and have a common voice when the FDA brings up new guidance documents, and a common voice when things might get proposed in state capitols or in Congress that we need to have a voice on," said Stroever

"Through the Tissue Policy Group, processors have come together to work with the government and others on major issues," said Dan Shires of LifeLink. "It's taken the place of the regulatory affairs group. It's been a good thing."

"The larger tissue banks in the industry were probably under more scrutiny from the FDA than the smaller members were in the past," said Lou Barnes, "so there is a lot more engagement with the government through the Tissue Policy Group now than there ever has been."

Leadership and Oversight

The AATB has exhibited new leadership on a number of other fronts, such as in expanding tissue services. One of the first incidents that highlighted the need occurred after the 2000/2001 New Year's night club fire disaster in Volendam, Holland in which the need for allograft skin to treat over six burn patients far exceeded the ability and available allograft supplies of European tissue banks. Nine months later, the United States received its own wake-up call on September 11, 2001. Within minutes of the attack the AATB's Skin Council were exchanging emails with each other regarding the possible need for allograft skin for potential burn victims. Unable to reach the Washington office due to a communications glut, the Skin Council began developing "what if" scenarios, and the logistical coordination of efforts in order to obtain an inventory of the amount of available allograft skin in both the immediate and short term, and to prevent a potential run on the currently available inventory by hospitals looking to bolster their existing inventories. The extent of the devastation limited injuries, but since then there has been a push, though the formation of the AATB's Emergency Preparedness Group to help localities stateside and around the world when a catastrophic event, like a fire or explosion, has created a need for allograft skin to victims.

Skin Allograft Material

Today, the AATB's Emergency Preparedness Task Force helps support locations around the world in times of crisis, such as the Imperial Sugar Refinery Fire in Port Wentworth, Georgia in 2008, where one million square centimeters of skin was made available to the severely burned victims. It also ascertains tissue is simply available in case of shortage or crisis. For the Obama inauguration on January 20, 2009, for instance, the Emergency Preparedness Task made certain there were over 7.5 million square centimeters available, and nearly 6.5 million square centimeters later that year for the G-20 summit in Pittsburgh. Anywhere there are earthquakes, fires, explosions or other catastrophes likely to require skin grafts for burn victims, the Task Force has been ready.

While the AATB continues core operations, such as updating standards, educating and certifying specialists, and accrediting tissue banks, new frontiers are constantly being explored. Dr. Hornicek pointed out that the AATB has taken a more scientific approach to donor screening and to the process of evaluating a survey with a new Donor Risk Assessment interview process and form (UDRAI).

"The Donor Risk Assessment is an interview process and involves several forms." said Brubaker. "We formed a group, and over eight years we ended up developing three different forms: one for an adult donor, one for a child donor and one for the birth mother of a child donor. We ask about medical history and travel history and behavioral risk history, just like when you donate blood. We have a similar questionnaire that can be used for any organ, eye or tissue donor. And we developed a couple of tools like guidance documents and flow charts for managing the questions and dealing with the answers."

A New Direction from the Top

In 2012, the AATB decided to seek a leader who could guide the Association in its new "trade organization" style structure. "We were looking for a day-to-day leader for the association that could accelerate our progress," said incoming Chair Lou Barnes. "Frank Wilton was that person. He came from a prominent healthcare industry trade association, and he surrounded himself with people with the same mindset. We have only looked forward since Frank's hire, a great success."

"He and his team have taken us to new heights. We've had much more success with our efforts with the FDA, which has secured a better future for us. I think the organization runs better as a result of that close connection between the Tissue Policy Group and Frank and the staff. Frank's done a great job."

"Frank Wilton did his homework when he first came on board as the CEO of AATB." said Diane Wilson of CTS, in 2009 the first female and first non-physician to assume the presidency of the AATB.

"He visited tissue banks one right after another. Met with them, talked with the CEOs and their staffs and listened to the tissue bank's concerns. Frank heard the banks saying that they wanted stronger voices with politicians, we need a policy group, we need more donor input. Frank made it happen. We have gone leaps with him."

Increased Emphasis on Accreditation and Other Administrative Changes

The Board of Governors has also become more proactive in recent years. "During my first stint on the Board of Governors we tackled Association membership structure," said Lou Barnes, "We increased the total membership talent pool by granting membership slots to accredited banks tied to their size. This greatly increased the number of members now eligible to volunteer, which may lead to help in filling committee appointment slots."

According to research, 98 percent of all adults have heard about organ donation and 86 percent have heard of tissue donation.[32] Ninety percent of Americans say they support donation, but only 30 percent know the essential steps to take to be a donor.[33] To address these needs in awareness and communications, the AATB has begun to pay a lot more attention to public relations, and formed the Communications Committee to share best practices among tissue-banking communications professionals.

The board has also increased office personnel to provide for growth, and in 2014, it moved the organization into larger offices in McLean, Va. It also added staff, most significantly, four full-time employees to handle accreditation. Today, the AATB accreditation program remains the only private accreditation program for tissue banks in the U.S "We get accredited every three years," said Lori Brigham president and chief executive officer of the Washington Regional Transplant Community (WRTC), the OPO in the greater D.C. area. "The information is constantly evolving—a new virus, like West Nile, a new donor risk assessment tool—so we have to keep current. The accreditation process helps us do that."

Individual certification remains the highest of priorities. Nearly 5,700 professionals have been awarded the CTBS or CRCS certification. "Today it's harder, because people often only know one specialty, but the test covers knowledge in general: donor screening, recovery, quality, processing, distribution," said Applegate. "We have talked about advanced testing in sub-specialties, but for now people have to pass the whole test. Also, today you have to apply the standards to a scenario. It requires critical thinking. And people's jobs may depend on them passing the test."

Today the tested subject areas are (1) donor screening and testing, (2) recovery, (3) processing, (4) quality assurance, and (5) distribution. Those who pass receive their Certified Tissue Banking Specialist (CTBS) certification. Between 1995 and 1997, the reproductive professionals were provided a different certification exam and designation called the Certified Reproductive Cryotechnologist Specialist (CRCS).

Over the last 40 years, the AATB has created a profession out of helping people improve and even save the lives of others. "I think that the AATB has done a marvelous job balancing that very, very human side," said Diane Wilson. "It's about the donors and supporting them and giving them that link to further transplants with tissues, and at the same time making the graft more consistent, safer, and exactly what the clinician or surgeon was looking for. I think AATB has done an excellent job honoring the gift of tissue donation."

CHAPTER FOUR: TECHNOLOGY, GROWTH, CONSOLIDATION, AND GLOBALIZATION, 2000–PRESENT

A Gift of Life

All donation, be it tissue or organ, is a powerful and ongoing experience for both the donor family and the recipient.

In 1991, Linda and Don Chapman's daughter, Missy, suffered a freak tragic accident while playing, passing away at the age of eight. "We spent two days down at the CHKD hospital in Norfolk," Mrs. Chapman said, "waiting for her to come out of a coma. She never did." She was declared brain dead.

"I didn't even know about donation or what it was at the time," she continued. "It was fairly new, and kind of cutting edge. Missy became a donor because we had a coordinator from LifeNet come talk to us and explain to us what could happen if we chose to donate. He explained all about what organ and tissue donation meant. He was there comforting us through the whole time and explaining the process. I asked if we could bring my pastor in to the conversation and he said, 'yes.' What else could we do when she passed away but let her live through others?

"Missy donated her corneas which gave sight to two people. She donated her kidneys to two different people, a two-year old little girl and a 23-year old woman in North Carolina, who came off of dialysis because of Missy's donation. Her liver went to a ten-year old boy in New York. That became our legacy.

"When you see someone who has come right out of surgery and six weeks later they are as vibrant as ever, you are thinking, 'Are you kidding me? You were on death's bed?' The Gift of Donation brought health, healing and hope.

"We've developed friendships with a lot of recipients, but not specific to Missy's donation. When you are in that situation, it really doesn't matter. There are those family members of donors that want to know the recipients. They want to meet them… be a part of their lives. So today it is more common to make that union of donor family and recipient happen."

After Missy's donation, Mrs. Chapman wanted to educate the public about organ donation. At first, she volunteered at LifeNet and has now been working there for twelve years. She is currently a

A Gift of Life

receptionist in the Institute for Regenerative Medicine, but understanding her work and its mission, also helps out in many other ways.

"For the newly bereaved it is hard to let go of anything. You want to preserve all your memories, so I became part of Donor Family Services that teach new donor families how to create a tribute album to honor their loved one, or to make memory boxes so they can go home and say 'I've got this.' It helps us work through the grief process.

"I believe in my company's mission and am reminded every day to help others and save lives; I am driven by that and Missy's donation."

Epilogue: Looking Ahead

The AATB will continue to adhere to its traditional priorities of increasing the availability of tissues for transplant, caring for donors and donor families, and supporting tissue-banking activities that lead to the provision of safe tissue of high quality for recipients. It will continue fulfilling those missions through publishing the latest standards, guidance documents, and protocols, devoting energy and resources to education, training and individual certification, accrediting tissue banks, working closely with the FDA and other agencies and organizations, and serving as an unofficial watchdog for the profession.

"Our Association," said incoming Chair Lou Barnes, "is grounded in the science of safety, efficacy and ethical behavior. With every donation we have one, and only one, opportunity to do right by the donor and his or her family."

Lou Barnes

Within those priorities and parameters, however, the future will bring a great deal of change. "Emerging infectious diseases are a significant concern," said AATB President and CEO Frank Wilton. "What is the next Ebola or Zika virus and, if this is deemed to be a potential risk to the recipient, will our accredited institutions have access to tests with appropriate specificity and sensitivity to ensure that we can adequately screen donors for eligibility?

"Secondly, as regenerative medicine, stem cell therapies and new tissue types evolve, will the regulatory science keep up with advances in tissue technology so patients have access to novel, breakthrough tissue treatments."

In this arena, Bud Brame, vice president of tissue services at LifeNet, cites "the development of de-cellularization to make tissues more biocompatible, and technologies that allow bone and tendon grafts to be stored more easily at room temperatures," as particularly exciting areas of research.

Dr. Ross Wilkins with AlloSource notes that the research on signals that trigger the transformation of stem cells into various kinds of tissue as particularly exciting. "We are very good at turning stem cells into bone," he says, "but we are not good at turning it into cartilage. We don't know the signal. There is a lot of research in that area."

The future is promising, yes, but it won't be a free ticket, says Dan Shires of LifeLink. "Science is giving us an opportunity to understand biologics better, but bringing something new is going to be increasingly difficult and expensive."

Bone Allograft Material

"The next step for us," said Lou Barnes, "is to engage the scientific community and get more bench scientists at universities and other research institutions interested in our work, our passion of serving donors and transplant recipients. Our mission needs them, and we need them to join our association that saves and enhances lives every day."

Turning from scientific research, collaboration will remain a focus. In recent years, the AATB has been in discussions with a division within the Office of the Assistant Secretary for Health regarding establishment of a system that could address any emergency needs for tissue—not just skin—due to a catastrophic event. The AATB has also collaborated with The Joint Commission (TJC) to further develop their standards that promote the safe handling of tissue. "We did a lot with TJC in helping them to align their standards with our standards and expectations," said Brubaker, "and they were very receptive."

Frank Wilton notes that this kind of "collaboration with FDA will continue to be crucial. We look forward to working constructively with the agency as they craft future guidances and regulation."

"The AATB will continue to communicate with FDA," says Brame "but the FDA doesn't know what it doesn't know. We need to focus on continual education."

To that same point, Doug Wilson, executive vice president at LifeNet, references the increasing complexity of the field and says, "I think a shift is under way. With such rapidly advancing technologies, the government can't possibly keep up. The FDA will have to rely more and more on private or non-governmental organizations like the AATB."

Thinking geographically, Wilton notes, "More of our banks are expanding internationally. While tissue banking evolved more quickly here in the U.S., there are significant opportunities for our accredited banks overseas. The challenge for our banks that expand internationally will continue to be the quest for the global harmonization of regulations and practices." Indeed, the figures back up Wilton's point. In the United States in 2007, for instance, 48 tissue banks distributed 2,110,200 tissue grafts from 30,380 donors and distributed tissue to more than 45 other countries.[34] "But," notes Wilton, "how will we harmonize our regulations with Germany's, or Spain's, or any other country's?"

Regarding the tissue-banking community, the conventional wisdom is that the consolidation of small tissue banks into larger ones that has occurred in recent years will continue. "More and more today tissue banks need a large and diverse staff of employees… engineers, administrators, high level quality professionals," says Diane Wilson. "As time goes on, it becomes increasingly difficult for a small processor to manage the extensive oversight of regulations, validations, equipment, and certifications. In other words, consolidation will likely continue in order to achieve economies of scale necessary to meet tomorrow's increasing demands.

From the perspective of the executive director's office, Wilton is acutely aware that the recent changes to the Bylaws instituted by the membership have lead to a tripling of AATB individual members. "As an organization, we need to continue to identify ways to engage these new members into the various committees, councils and other volunteer opportunities available within AATB. As the number of accredited banks increases, the CTBS program continues to grow and the need for basic scientific research expands, how will AATB generate the resources necessary to support these vital programs?"

In other words, the future is bright and the opportunities to make a difference in the lives of recipients will increase in ways we do not even yet comprehend. The tissue-banking community can expect administrative, financial, regulatory, collaborative and clinical changes. The common axiom that the only constant is change applies perfectly to tissue banking, and the AATB has throughout its history, helped its members adapt.

The Far Future

The far future, that beyond the

immediate horizon, will be one of even more change. "Stem cells and particular other types of cells are going to be cultured in volume," suggests Dr. Robert Stevenson. "And we will be able to put them in a 3-D printer and produce an organ or tissue. We have already had a reasonable amount of success in doing things such as making noses and ears with cartilage cells."

"It is possible that with cellular advances, within 20 years' time, there will be no need to have any extensive tissue retrieval activities from deceased donors," he continues. "We will have banks of cells and cell lines in vitro. A person will bank these cells and then use them primarily for the construction of replacements."

Dr. Wilkins agrees, and suggests that those cells will be one's own. "There's no longer such a premium on embryonic stem cells because there are stem cells in everyone's body." Autologous and allograft cell treatment like this would circumvent what Dr. Wilkins says in the biggest obstacle at the moment; rejection, especially in vascularized tissues. "We can transplant a lot of things," he says. "That's not the issue. Rejection of living composite tissue is. People used to think of us as mechanics, replacing parts. As time goes on, we will increasingly become gardeners, tending and nurturing the growth of cells and tissue."

Central Principle

"The most important thing of all," says Glenn Greenleaf of Acelity, "and I say this often in my work today—is to honor the gift. Remember that! It is up to those of us in the AATB to make sure that people never forget, because someone died for this gift. We have to honor that."

Diane Wilson concurs. "It is our responsibility to honor every part of the donor's gift, maximize that gift and touch as many recipients as we possibly can."

Tissue banking is a life-saving bridge constructed by science that links death with life. By their very work, tissue-banking professionals provide meaning to what can seem to be a meaningless and painful tragedy to a family of someone who has passed.

For the recipients of life-giving tissue, it means sometimes not just an enhanced life, but that a father or mother will be there to help their children grow up, or that young people will live a full life that otherwise would have ended. The reality to both sides is almost too profound to comprehend.

But these life-saving and life-changing surgeries would not have taken place without hundreds of professionals, starting with Dr. Kenneth Sell, who built the Association that allowed them to build on one another's knowledge, and share information with outside organizations.

Because of the vision of Dr. Sell and the other founders, because of the hard work of the members of the AATB, and because of the generous donations of thousands of tissue donors and tissue donor families, millions of lives have been changed.

Appendix

AATB Chairs

2015-2017	Dr. Daniel Schultz
2013-2015	Kevin Cmunt

AATB Past Presidents

2011-2013	David Smith, M.D.
2009-2011	Diane Wilson, B.S.N., M.S.N./M.H.A., R.N.
2007-2009	Francis Hornicek, M.D., Ph.D.
2005-2007	James H. Forsell, Ph.D.
2003-2005	Duke Kasprisin, M.D.
2001-2003	Samuel H. Doppelt, M.D.
1999-2001	Richard J. Kagan, M.D.
1997-1999	Michael J. Joyce, M.D.
1995-1997	S. Randolph May, Ph.D.
1993-1995	D. Ted Eastlund, M.D.
1991-1993	Charles B. Cuono, M.D., Ph.D.
1989-1991	John R. Kateley, Ph.D.
1987-1989	William W. Tomford, M.D.
1985-1987	Kenneth W. Sell, M.D., Ph.D.
1983-1985	Gary Friedlaender, M.D.
1981-1983	Harold T. Meryman, M.D.
1980-1981	Kenneth W. Sell, M.D., Ph.D.
1977-1979	Kenneth W. Sell, M.D., Ph.D.

Endnotes

1. Wang, Mary H. "FDA Oversight of the Tissue Bank Industry." Harvard Law School, 2002. Web. (https://dash.harvard.edu/bitstream/handle/1/8852205/tissue_donation_paper_final_with%20abstract.html?sequence=2)

2. American Association of Tissue Banks. "2007 Annual Survey Results for AATB-Accredited Tissue Banks in the United States." McLean, VA: AATB, 2010. Print.

3. *The Golden Legend or Lives of the Saints.* Compiled by Jacobus de Voragine. Trans. William Caxton. Ed. F.S. Ellis. London: Temple Classics, 1900. Web. (http://legacy.fordham.edu/halsall/basis/goldenlegend/GoldenLegend-Volume5.asp#Cornelius)

4. Nather, Aziz, Norimah Yusof, and Nazly Hilmy. *Allograft Procurement, Processing and Transplantation: A Comprehensive Guide for Tissue Banks.* Singapore: World Scientific Publishing, 2010. Web. (http://media.axon.es/pdf/82651_2.pdf)

5. "Organ Transplantation." LiveOnNY. *LiveOnNY,* Inc. Web. (http://www.liveonny.org/all-about-transplantation/tissue-transplanthistory/)

6. Narayan, R.P. "Development of Tissue Bank." *Indian Journal of Plastic Surgery* 45.2 (2012): 396-402. Web. (http://www.ncbi.nlm.nih.gov/pmc/articles/PMC3495391/)

7. Nugent, D., D. Meirow, P.F. Brook, Y. Aubard, and R.G. Gosden. "Transplantation in Reproductive Medicine: Previous Experience, Present Knowledge and Future Prospects." *Human Reproduction Update* 3.3 (1997): 267-280. Web. (http://humupd.oxfordjournals.org/content/3/3/267.full.pdf)

8. Shedd, Donald P. and Loring W. Pratt. "James Barrett Brown (1899-1971), Head and Neck Surgeon of a Half-Century Ago." *JAMA Otolaryngology—Head & Neck Surgery* 128.3 (2002): 233-235. Web. (http://archotol.jamanetwork.com/article.aspx?articleid=482797)

9. "History of Milk Banking." *Mothers' Milk Bank of North Texas.* Mother's Milk Bank of North Texas. Web. (http://www.texasmilkbank.org/history-milk-banking)

10. Narayan, R.P. "Development of Tissue Bank."

11. In the late 1940s and early 1950s, bone banks began to develop in the U.S. and abroad. In the United States, bone banks were usually developed in hospitals by surgeons for the use of their own patients: Stuck and Dandridge, San Antonio, Texas, 1950; Gordon and Welsh, Louisville, Kentucky, 1951; Cloward, Honolulu, Hawaii, 1952; Tucker, Houston, Texas, 1953; Wilson Hospital for Special Surgery, New York, New York, 1946; Rountree, Oklahoma City, Oklahoma, 1950; LeCocq, Seattle, Washington, 1948. Banks were similarly organized abroad at the Karolinska Institute in Stockholm, Sweden, 1948 (Huh); Paris, France, 1948 (Arviset and Judet); British General (Army) Hospital, U.K., 1948 (Henry); Edinburgh, Scotland, 1953 (Duthie); Department of Surgery Wilhelmina-Gasthuis, University of Amsterdam (xenografts), 1954 (Kingma). Food and Drug Administration; Mid-Atlantic Region Tissue Course, February 1-3, 1995, Presentation by Jeanne C. Mowe, Executive Director, American Association of Tissue Banks, pg. 2

12. Strong, Douglas Michael. "The US Navy Tissue Bank: 50 Years on the Cutting Edge." *Cell and Tissue Banking* 1.1 (2000): 9-16. Web. (https://www.researchgate.net/publication/8452570_The_US_Navy_Tissue_Bank_50_years_on_the_cutting_edge)

13. Following lengthy legal consultations and the advice of surgeons and physicians, procedures were established to aseptically recover bone and tissue from cadavers using extensive screening protocols. A facility needed to be established in order to do such recoveries under aseptic conditions. This idea became a reality in May 1951, when a new tissue bank suite was opened in the Naval Medical School. The postmortem excision of tissue under aseptic conditions for tissue banking was first performed on May 28, 1951. By the end of that year, the Tissue Bank had performed 15 aseptic postmortem tissue excisions and was regularly storing and shipping freeze-dried bone and refrigerated skin stored in nutrient media. (Strong, Douglas Michael. "The US Navy Tissue Bank.")

14. In 1951, the first clinical evaluations of arterial allografts were carried out at the Naval Hospital in Bethesda (MacPherson et al. 1951). Their success resulted in such a demand for arterial grafts that the Navy sent out a request to all naval hospitals for assistance in procurement. (Strong, Douglas Michael. "The US Navy Tissue Bank.")

15. Smith, Audrey U., Ed. *Current Trends in Cryobiology.* New York: Springer Science+Business Media, 1970. Web. (https://books.google.com/books?id=EETjBwAAQBAJ&pg=PA158&lp%20g=PA158&dq=union+%20carbide+cryobiology&source=bl&ots=iHD2j%20BAid4&sig=hDqjGvYvi8DhfNvXlHgMDRjsMXc&hl=en&sa=X&ved=0ahUK%20EwiauL_gevLAhUO1mMKHTsoDw4Q6AEIKTAD#v=onepage&q=uni%20on%20carbide%20cryobiology&f=false)

16. Ricks, Sharon. "NIDDK Mourns Louis A. Cohen." *The NIH Record* 48 (19 Nov. 1996): n. page. Web. (https://nihrecord.nih.gov/newsletters/11_19_96/obits.htm)

Endnotes

17. "DeGett's Organ Transplant Bill Becomes Law." *Chief Deputy Whip Diana DeGette: Representing the 1st District of Colorado.* 20 Oct. 2008. Web. (https://degette.house.gov/media-center/press-releases/degettes-organ-transplant-bill-becomes-law-0)

18. "Liver Allocation and Distribution Policy." *Health Resources & Services Administration.* U.S. Department of Health and Human Services. Web. (https://optn.transplant.hrsa.gov/)

19. "Nation's Largest Tissue Bank to Acquire Assets of American Red Cross Tissue Services." *PR Newswire.* 15 Nov. 2004. Web. (http://www.prnewswire.com/news-releases/nations-largest-tissue-bank-to-acquire-assets-of-american-red-cross-tissue-services-division-75412807.html)

20. Rogers, Martha F. et al. "Guidelines for Preventing Transmission of Human Immunodeficiency Virus Through Transplantation of Human Tissue and Organs." *Morbidity and Mortality Weekly Report* 43.RR-8 (1994): 1-17. Web. (http://www.cdc.gov/mmwr/preview/mmwrhtml/00031670.htm)

21. "Is This Product a Medical Device?" *U.S. Food and Drug Administration.* U.S. Department of Health and Human Services. 12 Sep. 2014. Web. (http://www.fda.gov/%20MedicalDevices/DeviceRegulationandGuidance/Overview/%20ClassifyYourDevice/ucm051512.htm)

22. Joyce, Michael J. "American Association of Tissue Banks: A Historical Reflection Upon Entering the 21st Century." *Cell and Tissue Banking* 1.1 (2000): 5-8. Print.

23. Warner, J.H. and K.C. Zoon. "The View from the Food and Drug Administration." Younger, S., M. Anderson, and R. Schapiro, eds. *Transplanting Human Tissue: Ethics, Policy, and Practice.* New York, NY: Oxford University Press, Inc., 2004. 71-85. Print.

24. Studies have corroborated this risk. Tissue and Cell Donation: An Essential Guide, edited by Scott Brubaker and Ted Eastlund, among others, stated "In parts of the United States, funeral home recoveries became more active in the 1990s and into the 2000s, as demand for tissue increased... This type of program increased tissue available to some tissue banks, but it is felt by some to have been a system ripe for misuse and abuse."

    Warwick, Ruth, Deidre Fehily, Scott Brubaker, and Ted Eastlund, eds. Tissue and Cell Donation: An Essential Guide. West Sussex, UK: Wiley-Blackwell, 2009. Print.

25. An Interim Final Rule on human tissue intended for transplantation. "Good Tissue Practice (CGTP) Final Rule Questions and Answers." *U.S. Food and Drug Administration.* U.S. Department of Health and Human Services. 5 May 2009. Web. (http://www.fda.gov/BiologicsBloodVaccines/TissueTissueProducts/QuestionsaboutTissues/ucm102994.htm)

26. U.S. Department of Health and Human Services, Food and Drug Administration. "Eligibility Determination for Donors of Human Cells, Tissues, and Cellular Tissue-Based Products." *Code of Federal Regulations* Title 21. Web. (http://www.fda.gov/OHRMS/DOCKETS/98fr/97N-484S-nfr0001.pdf)

27. U.S. Department of Health and Human Services, Food and Drug Administration. "Proposed Approach to Regulation of Cellular and Tissue-Based Products." 28 Feb. 1997. Web. (http://www.fda.gov/downloads/BiologicsBloodVaccines/Guidance%20ComplianceRegulatoryInfor%20mation/Guidances/Tissue/UCM062601.pdf)

28. "Organ Procurement Organizations." *organdonor.gov.* Health Resources & Services Administration, U.S. Department of Health & Human Services. Web. (http://www.organdonor.gov/materialsresources/materialsopolist.html)

29. Joyce, Michael J., Scott A. Brubaker, A. Seth Greenwald, and Christine S. Heim. "Musculoskeletal Allograft Tissue Safety: Improving Safety by Knowing That Your Allograft Has Not Been Recalled or Quarentined." American Academy of Orthopaedic Surgeons, 77th Annual Meeting. New Orleans, LA. 9-13 March 2010. Web. (http://aatb.org/aatb/files/ccLibraryFiles/Filename/000000001069/Tissue%20Safety%202010%20AAOS%20Brochure.pdf)

30. Institute of Medicine (U.S.), Committee on Organ Procurement and Transplantation Policy. *Organ Procurement and Transplantation: Assessing Current Policies and the Potential Impact of the DHHS Final Rule.* Washington, D.C.: National Academies Press, 1999. Web. (http://www.ncbi.nlm.nih.gov/books/NBK224642/)

31. AATB. AATB Bulletin 7.18 (2007): 1. Print.

32. "Statistics." *Midwest Transplant Network.* Midwest Transplant Network, 2012. Web. (http://www.mwtn.org/stats)

33. "Organ, Eye, and Tissue Donation Statistics." Donate Life America. Donate Life America, 2016. Web. (https://www.donatelife.net/statistics/)

34. Fishman, Jay A., Melissa A. Greenwald, and Paolo A. Grossi. "Transmission of Infection With Human Allografts: Essential Considerations in Donor Screening." *Clinical and Infectious Diseases* 55.5 (2012): 720-272. Web. (http://cid.oxfordjournals.org/content/early/2012/06/15/cid.cis519)

Permissions

1 Courtesy of Georgetown University School of Medicine

2 With permission of Springer; Strong, Douglas Michael. "The US Navy Tissue Bank: 50 Years on the Cutting Edge." *Cell and Tissue Banking* 1.1 (2000):9-16., pg. 10

5 With permission of Springer; Strong, Douglas Michael. "The US Navy Tissue Bank: 50 Years on the Cutting Edge." *Cell and Tissue Banking* 1.1 (2000):9-16. pg. 11

8 Courtesy of Gary Friedlaender, M.D.

10 Courtesy of LifeNet Health. Used with permission.

12 Courtesy of Mr. and Mrs. Jesse McGinley

30 Courtesy of the family of Jeanne Mowe

37 Courtesy of Theodore Eastlund, M.D.

45 Courtesy of LifeNet Health. Used with permission.

60 Courtesy of Ashleigh Deal

72 Courtesy of the Association of Organ Procurement Organizations

77 Courtesy of Acelity

85 Courtesy of Mr. Lou Barnes

86 Courtesy of LifeNet Health. Used with permission.

Index

A

AABB. *See* American Association of Blood Banks
AATB. *See* American Association of Tissue Banks
AATB Standards for Tissue Banking
  disease transmission, 66
  FDA regulations, 51
  first publication, 20
  updating and improving, 41, 64–65
AATB *Technical Manual*, 20
  accreditation program
  committee for, 27–28
  emphasis on, 78–79
  foreign accredited tissue banks, 73
  incentives for, 42–43
  inspection program, 43
  peer audits for, 43
  tissue bank, 64–65
  See also certification
Accredited Tissue Bank Council (ATBC), 37
Acelity (formerly LifeCell)
  blood and tissue preservation focus, 31–32
  commercial processing, 54
  consolidation, 69
  Glenn Greenleaf, 21, 89
  adverse outcome reporting, 68

allograft heart valves 45-46, 55
  FDA classification of heart valves, 45–46
  tissue-device separation, 54
AlloSource
  consolidation, 69, 72
  creation of, 32
  growth of tissue banking, 31
  institutional and monitoring needs, 58
  international footprint of, 70
  Osteotech competition, 54
  See also Mile High Transplant Bank
American Academy of Orthopaedic Surgeons (AAOS), 57
American Association of Blood Banks, 25, 56–57, 59
American Association of Tissue Banks
  collaboration, 49–50, 57, 60
  Communications Committee, 78–79
  councils of, 16
  Emergency Preparedness Group/Task Force, 76–77
  future concerns, 85–86
  governance changes, 58–59
  harmonization of standards, 27–28
  HIV screening workgroup, 38
  leadership changes, 35, 74–77

Medical Advisory Committee, 36
  membership, 88
  non-profit status, 74
  organizational structure, 17
  principles and priorities, 85, 89
  quality and regulatory matters, 74
  Technical Manual, 20
  See also accreditation program; certification; tissue banking; tissue/organ donation
American Association of Tissue Banks history
  1949-1976, 1–14
  1976-1987, 15–30
  1987-2000, 31–60
  2000 to present, 63–83
  chairs and presidents, 91
  founding members, 8, 15–16
American Burn Association (ABA)
  Burn Care Resources Directory, 66
  collaboration with AATB, 57
  media misinformation, 65
American Dental Association (ADA), 65
American Orthopaedic Society for Sports Medicine (AOSSM), 57
American Red Cross, 37–38

American Red Cross Tissue Services, 40
amniotic tissue donation, 60
Anderson, Bill
  Eastern Virginia Tissue Bank, 9–10, 21
  LifeNet Health/Transplant Services, 21, 33
Applegate, Paula, 40, 79
"Approach to Regulation of Cellular & Tissue-Based Products," 51
ARC Tissue Services, 39
arterial allografting, 4
Asian Pacific Association of Tissue Banks, 73
autologous tissue and cell banking, 1, 89

B

Barnes, Lou
  government engagement, 63, 75
  Jeanne Mowe influence, 56
  membership increases, 78
  principles and priorities, 85
  safety and standard setting, 63
  scientific community engagement, 86
  trade organization orientation, 77
Bierbaum, Russ
  cooperation among tissue banks, 59

Index

education and certification, 23
FDA involvement in tissue banking, 49–50
inspection program, 43
blood technology (private sector), 5–6
Bottenfield, Helen, 1–2, 10, 21–22
Bottenfield, Scott, 39
Brame, Bud, 86–87
Brigham, Lori, 79
British Human Tissue Act, 6–7
Brodine, C. E., 19
Brubaker, Scott
 Ebola and West Nile screening, 67
 international recognition of AATB, 74
 Joint Commission tissue standards, 42, 65, 87
 proactive approach to safety, 63–64
 tissue management hand book, 56–57
 traceability and tracking issues, 68–69
 UDRAI process, 77

C

Campagnari, David
 accreditation program, 28, 42
 bone marrow storage, 9
 FDA and tissue safety, 46
 global recognition of AATB, 74
 joining AATB, 22
Center for Biologics Evaluation and Research (CBER), 50
Centers for Disease Control and Prevention (CDC)
 donor screening criteria, 38–39, 67
 guidance documents for clinicians, 69
 HIV transmission reported, 46–48
 standards update and expansion, 64
 Tissue Action Plan, 51–52
certification
 standardized education for, 22–23, 40
 subject areas tested, 79
 See also accreditation program
Certified Reproductive Cryotechnologist Specialist (CRCS), 79
Certified Tissue Banking Specialist (CTBS), 39, 79
Chapman, Missy, donation of tissue, 81–82
commercial processors, 52–55
Community Tissue Services (CTS), 32–33, 70
Comprehensive Guidelines for Prevention of HIV Transmission from Transplanted Organs and Tissues, 38–39
consolidation of tissue banks, 69–72, 88
cornea donations, vii, 37
CryoLife, Inc., 13, 33, 54–55, 70
cryopreservation, 16, 46
Cuono, Charles B., 35, 39
Cycyota, Tom, 73

D

Dayton Regional Tissue Bank. *See* Community Tissue Services (CTS)
Department of Health and Human Services (DHHS), 23, 25–26, 57
disease transmission. *See* infectious diseases
donation of tissue/organs. *See* tissue/organ donation
Donor Alliance, 26, 72
Donor Family Services, 82
Dunn, Sue, 26, 72

E

Eastern Virginia Tissue Bank (EVTB), 2, 9–10, 33
Eastlund, D. Ted, 36–37, 41–42, 54
Ebola virus, 66–67
Erickson, Mike, tissue donation, 29
European Association of Tissue Banks (EATB), 73
Eye Bank Association of America (EBAA), 50, 57

F

Fauci, Anthony S., 47
"Final Rule and Guidance Document for Human Tissue Intended for Transplantation," 51
Food and Drug Administration (FDA)
 AATB anticipation of regulation by, 27
 guidance documents, 51–52
 HIV screening procedures, 38–39
 Interim Final Rule publication, 50
 regulation of tissues, 27
 relationship with AATB, 44–45, 48–49
for-profit tissue processors. *See* commercial processors
freeze drying tissues, 4
Friedlander, Gary E., 8, 11, 18

G

Gift of Hope Organ & Tissue Donor Network, 72
Gitelis, Steve, 32
globalization, 73, 87
Glowacki, Julie, 16

Index

Gore, Al. *See* National Organ Transplant Act
Greenleaf, Glenn
growth of tissue banking, 31
harmonization of standards, 27
honor the gift principle, 89
tissue banking culture, 21–22
Guidelines for Tissue Banking, 20

H

Hatch, Orin, 24
Health Care Finance Administration (HFCA), 39
Health Resources and Services Administration (HRSA), 39
heart valves (allograft). *See* allograft heart valves
HIV testing, 26, 66–67
Hornicek, Francis
   donor screening, 77
   international expansion, 73
   trade organization model, 74
   updating and extending standards, 64, 66
"Human Tissue Intended for Transplantation," 50
Hurwitz, Richard L., 39
Hyatt, George W.
   Father of American Tissue Banking, 3
   photograph of, viii

vision of allografting, 1–3, 8
See also Navy Tissue Bank

I

infectious diseases, 38–39, 51–52, 66–67, 85–86
Iowa Donor Network, 72

J

Joint Commission on Accreditation, Health Care and Certification (TJC)
   adverse reaction reporting, 41–42
   expansion of standards by, 65
   standards for safe tissue handling, 86–87
Joyce, Michael J.
   accreditation and inspections, 27, 43–44
   commercial processors, 53–55
   donor screening, 24, 26
   FDA collaboration, 50, 52
   imported tissue sales, 48
   mission and governance analysis, 58–59
   MTF established, 34
   standards and protocol established, 16–18, 21, 41

K

Kagan, Richard J.
   accreditation and inspection

programs, 43
   FDA relationship, 48–49
   HIV testing, 38
   media misinformation, 65–66
   personnel certification, 39–40
   skin banking, 22
Kainer, Marion, 66
Kinetics Concepts Incorporated, 69
Korean War, 2, 5

L

legal issues and milestones
   FDA classification challenge, 45–46
   National Organ Transplant Act, 24–25
   tissue procurement, 6–7
   transplantation, 15–16
   Uniform Anatomical Gift Act, 7–9
LifeCell. *See* Acelity
LifeGift, 72
LifeLink Tissue Bank, 26, 33, 70–71, 73
LifeNet, Missy Chapman donation, 81–82
LifeNet Transplant Services, 10, 31, 33, 39, 58, 71

M

MacEwen, William, iii
Malinin, Theodore I. (Ted), 9, 16, 33–34
May, S. Randolph (Randy), 22, 58
McGinley, Elijah and Walker, 12–13
Medical Advisory Committee, 36
Meryman, Harold T., 4, 20
Meyer, Henry (Hank), 45
Miami Tissue Bank, 16
Michigan Tissue Bank, 54
Mid-America Transplant, 72
Mile High Transplant Bank, 9, 20, 32. *See also* AlloSource
Miller, Bill, 37–38
MiMedx, Inc., 31, 71
Mother's Milk Bank, 20
Mowe, Jeanne, 20, 29, 41–42, 52, 56, 58–59
Musculoskeletal Transplant Foundation (MTF), 31, 34, 39, 58, 63, 71

N

National Cancer Institute, 6–7
National Conference of Commissioners on Uniform State Laws, 7
National Heart, Lung, and Blood Institute (NHLBI), 39

Index

National Kidney Foundation, 8
National Marrow Donor Program, 9
National Organ and Tissue Donation Initiative, 57
National Organ Transplant Act (NOTA), 24–25
National Research Institute, 7
National Task Force on Organ Transplantation, 25
Naval Medical Research Institute (NMRI), 4, 8, 47
Navy Tissue Bank (NTB), 1–6, 8–11, 16, 19, 46, 52
NIH tissue procurement program, 9–10
Norfolk General Hospital, 33

O

Ocular Council, 37
operating models tissue banking, 72
Organ Bank of Illinois, 32
organ donation. *See* tissue/organ donation
Organ Procurement and Transplantation Network, 25–26
organ procurement organizations (OPOs)
   donation initiatives, 57
   operation funding for, 25–26
   pooling of resources, 32

Osborne, Joel, 39, 42–43
Osteotech, 38–39, 54
Ostrander, James E., 16

P

Perry, Vernon P., 16
personnel training. *See* certification
private sector tissue banks, 9–11
procurement of tissue. *See* tissue/organ donation
professional certification. *See* certification
Project Notify (WHO), 68–69
Prolo, Donald, 16
"Proposed Approach to the Regulation of Cellular and Tissue-based Products," 51
Public Health Service (PHS), 26, 38

R

Reagan, Ronald, 25
regenerative medicine, 85–86
ReproTech, 40
Rigney, P. Robert, 59
RTI Surgical, Inc., 31, 34, 54, 71. *See also* University of Miami Tissue Bank
Rush University Medical Center, 32

S

Sandler, Jeff, 9
Sasso, John C., 16
Scientific and Technical Affairs Committee (STAC), 64
Sell, Kenneth W.
   expertise of, 8
   Father of the AATB, 47, 90
   FDA-AATB relationship, 44–45
   hiring of executive director, 56
   HIV testing and standards, 39
   NOTA testimony, 24
   photograph of, 14
   Tissue Bank Symposium, 18
   Washington D.C. clinician meeting, 15–16
Shires, Dan, 26, 75, 86
60 Minutes, 65–66
Skin Council emergency response, 76
skin substitute taskforce, 65
Society for Cryobiology, 6
Southeastern Organ Procurement Foundation, 11
stem cell research, 86, 88–89
Stevenson, Robert
   changes in tissue banking, 89
   early practitioners, 3
   freeze drying techniques, 4, 6
   goals of AATB, 15–16
   inspection program review, 44
   stem cell research, 89

   testimony on Gore-Hatch bill, 24
   tissue banking legal statutes, 7–9, 11
Stroever, Bruce, 53, 55, 63, 74–75
Systagenix, 69

T

Task Force on Organ Transplantation, 25–26
Tayo, Emmanuel, 43–44
The Joint Commission. *See* Joint Commission on Accreditation, Health Care and Certification
Tissue Action Plan (TAP), 51–52
Tissue and Cell Report, 36–37
Tissue Bank Symposium, 18–19
tissue banking
   competition in, 54
   cooperation in, 72–73
   culture of, 21
   donor screening risk factors, 48
   growth of, 31
   standards and protocols for, 10–11
   technology, 2, 85–86
   See also American Association of Tissue Banks (AATB) history
Tissue Policy Group, 74–75

Index

tissue/organ donation
  consent for, vii
  consolidation under OPOs, 26
  donor at-risk screening, 38–39
  formalization of consent, 6–8
  honoring the gift, 12–13, 29, 60, 81–82
  legal requirements, 57
  National Organ Transplant Act, 24–26
  organ-tissue donation combined, 21–22
  procurement and screening, 23–24
  tissue recovery, 4–5
  UAGA regulation, 11
Tomford, William, 1, 5–6, 15, 23, 45, 73
traceability and tracking, 68–69
transplantation, early history, iii–vii

U

UMTB Biomedical, Inc., 71–72
Uniform Anatomical Gift Act (UAGA), 7–9
Uniform Donor Card, 7
Uniform Donor Risk Assessment Interview (UDRAI), 67, 77
Union Carbide blood processing, 5–6
University of Miami Tissue Bank (UMTB), 9, 31, 34–35, 54. *See also* RTI Surgical, Inc.
Unyts, 72

V

van Meekeren, Job, iii
Vietnam War, 5–6, 8–9
Vincent, Monroe M., 16
Virginia Organ Procurement Organization (VOPA), 33–34
Virginia Tissue Bank (VTB). *See* Eastern Virginia Tissue Bank (EVTB)

W

Washington Regional Transplant Community (WRTC), 79
West Nile virus, 67
Western Association of Tissue Banks, 11
Wiggins, Jeff, 33
Wilkins, Ross
  autologous and allograft treatments, 89
  FDA/AATB partnership, 48, 52
  information sharing, 20
  organization of OPO Corporate Members, 32
  stem cell transformation, 86
Wilson, Diane
  AATB presidency of, 78
  consolidation of tissue banks, 88
  Dayton Regional Tissue Bank director, 32
  disease transmission, 24
  functions of AATB, 79
  hiring of Frank Wilton, 77–78
  honoring donor's gifts, 89
  human side of AATB, 80
Wilson, Doug, LifeNet Transplant Services, 87
Wilton, Frank, 77–78, 87
World Health Organization
  globalization, 73
  Project Notify, 68–69
World Union of Tissue Banking Associations, 73–74

Y

Year 2000 Plan, 35–36

Z

Zika virus, 66–67

Honoring the Gift: The American Association of Tissue Banks at 40